NOW
IS THE MOMENT

ALSO BY HAROLD RUGG

I. Books on American Life and Education

THAT MEN MAY UNDERSTAND, 1941

CULTURE AND EDUCATION IN AMERICA, 1931

THE GREAT TECHNOLOGY, 1933

THE CHILD-CENTERED SCHOOL, 1928
  (*in collaboration with Ann Shumaker*)

AMERICAN LIFE AND THE SCHOOL CURRICU-
    LUM, 1936

STATISTICAL METHODS APPLIED TO EDUCATION,
    1917

II. Books for Young Americans in Schools

MAN AND HIS CHANGING SOCIETY
  *A fourteen-volume series (1929-   ) based
  upon three experimental editions, The Social-
  Science Pamphlets (1922-1929)*

HAROLD RUGG

NOW
IS THE MOMENT

DUELL, SLOAN AND PEARCE · NEW YORK

Acknowledgment

Throughout this essay I have tried to make clear the vast extent to which it has been made possible by the work of distinguished students of western culture. I should like to add here, however, a brief note of deep personal indebtedness: first, to my research and editorial assistant, Ursula Reinhardt, during the time of writing . . . second, to my friend and colleague, F. Ernest Johnson, who read the manuscript and made suggestions of profound importance for its revision.

H. R.

Contents

Foreword

"GENTLEMEN—THIS IS OUR MOMENT—IF!"

A year ago, when I was writing the "war papers" that became the basis of this book, one major thesis gripped my mind. It was this: Now, in the 1940s, is our one strategic moment in the twentieth century to ban unemployment in peace time as well as in war and to take a vast stride forward toward a free, abundant, socially-secure society. No less than ten imperatives chorused the call "Now is the moment" . . . because at last we have reached the critical point—the optimum point—on the curve of industrial-democratic culture . . . and, because . . . there won't be another—in our Day. I documented the imperatives and the result is Chapter I of this book.

But, in company with liberals generally, I knew a year ago that there was a gigantic psychological-political "If!" and to implement it I wrote the four open letters of the concluding Chapter VIII under the caption "Gentlemen, This is Our Moment—If!" If . . . our people understand that *they must make up their minds* to work toward two goals, now, while the war is on against military fascism abroad. The first is to participate vigorously in bringing about an ordered world and a durable peace. The second is that they will not allow themselves to be engulfed by a giant depression in the post-war years; that they will run their social system on an abundance level without unemployment, in peace time as in war.

*Forebodings re the
Two Wars*

That warning "If" looms up today with even greater insistence than it did a year ago. As this book is locked up in press I sense that liberal Americans, while vigorously making and studying post-war plans, are gripped by two deep forebodings. First, The whole social trend of the winter of 1942-43 warns us—*there may not be time* to do what must be done. The War Abroad against foreign fascism may end before we are prepared for the War at Home against incipient American fascism. I mean the War for the Nine Freedoms—the war over work and security and social control and over vigorous American participation in world affairs. If we win the war abroad, but lose the war at home this horrible mass blood-letting will have been utterly in vain. In the winter of 1942-43 the liberals are not too sanguine about the chances of winning the war for the Nine Freedoms.

Our second foreboding is that the President and his liberal advisors will be beaten in their attempt to supplant European and Anglo-Saxon power-politics and geopolitics with a truly disarmed and democratic world order . . . to create a just and durable—not a vindictive, to-the-victor-belong-the-spoils—peace. We sense a strong counter current of restoration in our Atlantic world, a tendencious mood to restore monarchies to Europe's thrones . . . to restore Nazi-destroyed industrial and financial properties to pre-Hitler owners . . .

to restore the "free-market" as the basis of international trade . . . to restore colonies to pre-war imperialists . . . to restore *laissez faire* as the basis of production and distribution in all capitalistic countries. A counter-trend toward restoration, I say. There are many straws in the world wind that suggest this; these may not be connected but they suggest a marked trend, and liberals will do well to attend to them closely:

1. The Allied collaboration with the late Admiral Darlan and the political impasse in North Africa.
2. The acceptance by our War Department of Otto Hapsburg's proposal to create a fighting unit of "free" Austrians (plus portents like having the Department address him as "Otto of Austria"—instead of Hapsburg—and his current cordial reception in official Washington circles.)
3. The reiteration in the press of the practical wisdom of supporting the restoration of the House of Savoy against Mussolini.
4. The continued appeasement of Franco in Spain in spite of such omens as his fiftieth birthday telegram to Hitler praying for the success of Nazi arms.
5. The repeated declaration of the British Tory party in power that they shall "keep what they have" . . . Churchill's refusal to implement for India the principle of freedom in his Atlantic Charter . . . the failure and demotion of Sir Stafford Cripps, and similar phenomena.
6. The failure of our own leaders thus far to think in world terms, to make a World Charter that would embrace the billion colored peoples of China, India, and Indonesia as well as our Atlantic world.
7. The November 1942 elections and their aftermaths: the ominous signs of an America-First, back-to-normalcy Congress which will not hesitate to wipe out the

social gains of the past generation . . . and the accumulation of evidence that Vice President Wallace and his liberal associates are facing the defeat of their aspirations and plans and the extermination of their agencies for bringing about a free world.

This trend of events reveals itself at the very moment that word comes of Allied successes on every front—a tremendous Russian break-through, a toe-hold in Africa . . . a start back in the Pacific. With them looms up the spectre of the shortness of time to prepare our people for the War at Home which will start up again at the moment of the first armistice. Grave psychological questions arise. Are the people ready? Does early success on the Military front mean disaster on the social-psychological front? We need time—years of time—to build in the people the deep-seated conviction that they will make this the moment to lift the social world . . . to redirect social trend. Time enough to build resistance in the public mind to the propaganda of the isolationist, diehard Right and its vicious press. Time enough for a great campaign to arouse our people to an understanding that they can never go back to the old world of the pre-1930s . . . that they must go forward into a tense, dynamic, interdependent, and organized world.

This, I think, is the mood in which most liberals are doggedly going ahead and defending their designs for a new day.

HAROLD RUGG

NEW YORK
JANUARY 17, 1943

Tomorrow Is Today

There are moments in history when Tomorrow is Today,
When the mammoth glacier of social trend
    taking movement down the Valley of History
    can be diverted by men
Into pathways toward Tomorrow.

There are moments in history when Today is merely
    Today . . .
    inert, unchanging . . .
    When no mustering of energies
    Can prod man out of his inertia.

Then comes the moment when Tomorrow is Today,
When the flux is at free flow.
Then Man is Captain of his Soul
And the principle of the effective human act
    Works in a world at social crisis.

I'll say it this way, then—

    There is a favored moment . . . a place . . .
      and a mustering of energies
    Which, in unison, will produce an effective
      human act.

One

NOW IS THE MOMENT

It is my thesis that this is our moment. That by taking thought now . . . by focusing our total energies at the fulcrum and lifting together . . . we can move the social world.

Now is the moment to lift the social system up from the low rut of Exploitation onto the High Road toward the Great Tradition.

✓ ✓ ✓

By our moment I mean these current years—the 1940s, 50s, and 60s, and the years just passed—but especially the 1940s. To make the concept graphic, imagine the years from the turn into the twentieth century to, perhaps, the 1970s, marked off on a timeline. For some of us these years will measure the span of our lives—those ahead will be our mature and productive years; for our young people they are the thrilling formative ones. During these two generations we shall make the crucial social decision of modern history. We shall determine the kind of society that industrialized peoples around the globe will live in for generations to come . . . whether this shall be the century of the People's Peace or one of recurring and more devastating wars . . .

whether life shall be abundant or stunted, democratic or totalitarian, free or slave. To point emphatically to the transformational nature of this period I shall call it "The Great Transition."

We have not even a generation in which to make up our minds; we may not have a decade, for day by day events are shaping the data of future momentous decisions. This accents the war years—1941-44 . . . '45 . . . '46 . . . or what you will. They are crucial in more ways than in defeating the Axis, for we shall not merely be winning the war; we shall, in addition be winning or losing the peace. As we think and plan now, or drift without design, so shall we live throughout the rest of our lives.

TEN IMPERATIVES

No less than ten imperatives make this our moment.

I.

The first is that the nation's creative energies *are* being mustered. From all over the Place called America sensitive thinking people are stirring in a thousand communities and a great Structure of Design Leadership is forming. A key group, which already constitutes a potential national council of design and reconstruction, is assembling at Washington, but it is land-based on Regional Councils of the entire nation, on 48 State Planning Boards and on a vast number of Community Councils. There must be a center through which designs shall clear and the only practicable focus is the capital city. There a team of men of design and skilled executives grows, drawn from the top ranks of every phase of our culture. Every Valley is sending its talent—from Iowa the practical prophet of the Century of the Common Man . . . from Texas the successful business man, knowing by his feelings that "the plain people of this earth want to be wanted" . . . from the metropolis the experienced idealist social worker, builder of great public works, trusted confidant and adviser of the Prime Ministers of the democratic world . . . from private industry renowned engineers turned students and executives of the social system . . . from Harvard's chair of scholarship the economist who bursts academic chains to proclaim that "a people can afford whatever it can produce" . . . from Utah the successful banker, who believes with the production engineers and Columbia's designer of Capital Credit Banks that the bottle-neck of a stalled but potentially abundant society is finance-capitalism, and that the way shall be built to maintain the free flow of credit . . . from Wyoming a Senator who values national economic welfare more than good political fences . . . from top-leadership in the nation's manufacturing and railroad war production managers, liaison between government and business . . . from every university center the pick of creative design in the professional social sciences.

But—enough of cataloguing personnel; for more details look ahead to Chapter VI.

↗ ↗ ↗

Not only are the creative energies assembling; they are beginning to push the social system in the direction of a better world. Here, on the very threshold of consummation, is the thing we have dreamed of and pled for and work for—science in government . . . research in government . . . technical and administrative competence in government. In short, a government of social engineering, guided by brains and motivated by good will. In these attempts to implement the Four Freedoms —yes, the Nine Freedoms—are signs of the humane and efficient government we have so long craved but despaired of achieving. Here, then, is a true cross-section of the nation's talent—its poetry, its religion, as well as its science and technology. There's poetry . . . and religion . . . in Henry Wallace's "peace of the Common Man." There's more than efficient practicality in John Winant's "the drive for tanks must become the drive for houses." There is a poetic religious idealization of the good life that could be lived on our continent.

> There's poetry as well as pragmatism
>   and both are needed.
> Poetry can lift the world . . .
>   pragmatism can only direct it.
> Both are called for . . . Both are at hand.
> Men of Vision . . . Men of Competence.
>
> We must be careful, now . . .
>   not to belittle poetry
> Or we'll be left
> Well structured . . . well aimed
>   . . . with no engine force.
>   Inert.

2.

"The First Step Toward Virtue"

The second imperative making this our moment is that our fragile interdependent world society has reached such an impasse that we must do something promptly to help others, if for no other reason than to save ourselves. At the moment of the first major cessation of hostilities our people—or at least our leaders—will have made up their minds whether or not to sit at the head of the World's Council Table and to lead in the creation of new designs for a world of order. In accepting or rejecting world leadership in rehabilitation we shall be settling the question of continued war or peace at home for many years to come. Like the Two Wars from which the problem has sprung, the decision will have two foci— one global, the other domestic. But, like the singleness of the two fascist enemies in the Two Wars—the military fascism abroad and the economic-political fascism at home—so the two decisions that our people must make are really one.

Both private and public scholarship have raised danger signals of the imminence of a world-wide convulsion when hostilities cease. Hundreds of millions of people will face mass anarchy, starvation, and the rapine of vengeance-seeking peoples. The students agree that in order to avoid the destruction of all orderly processes of living a period of transition must take place—probably without any world peace conference or signed treaties— in which starving populations are fed, housed, and clothed, destroyed plants rebuilt, going ones switched over to peace-time production and workers put back to work. Millions of property relationships—now hopelessly tangled in Nazi-destroyed communities—must be re-established. Banditry and sporadic violence must be guarded against. The whole political structure of Europe must be re-organized.

This gigantic task of serving whole harassed continents can be managed only through the collaboration of
the United States, Great Britain, Russia, and China. But
our three allies will be well-nigh worn out themselves
and the burden of medicating a sick world will fall on
us. Our people must then decide whether to lead in
world reconstruction, whether we will give away without regard to lend-lease or reparations.

The experts of both the Right and the Left insist that
because of our giant resources and technically efficient
producing plant, our national economic system need not
collapse or even stall; our very assumption of the responsibility to rehabilitate the world will compel us to operate our farms and factories at near-peak load. And this
will contribute to a successful tapering off from war to
peace production. Only by producing full-tilt and giving
away billions to raise standards of living all over the
world can we build purchasing power in the hands of
our own people. Perhaps Senor de Madariaga did have
hold of a great truth when he exclaimed one day in the
course of a debate on international relations: "Well,
after all, hypocrisy may be the first step toward virtue."
At least we can say, with the psychologist and the artist,
that the making of the organic gesture—the practical
act—is the first step toward building intelligent understanding and appreciation in our people.

3.

We Fight Two Wars in One

And that brings me to the third imperative—the war
and what it has done to our minds. I'll say it this way:

Now is the moment—for we fight two wars—
  Tomorrow's war at home . . .
  Today's war abroad.
And these two wars are one.
To speak of the Peace now is to win the war
  —the two wars—
    Tomorrow's war at home . . .
    as well as Today's war abroad.

The war we fight abroad is a single Thirty Years War
—not a series of world wars . . . 1914-1918 . . .
1939-   . . . and decades of peace in between. For
thirty years the life of the peoples of Eurasia and Africa
has been constantly interrupted by the Dictators' armed
seizure of power and their undeclared war on civilization. War tension for thirty years. So we name it with
its proper name—the Thirty Years War.

As for the war at home—I mean the war over property and security and social control—it has been even
more continuous, more deeply rooted and world-wide
than the conflict abroad. Because of our necessary ab-
sorption now in the war abroad an apparent armistice
has come on the domestic front; when the military armistices succeed one another abroad, the war at home
will begin again.

If you do not agree that we fight an almost unbroken
war at home, recall, for example, the fourteen major depressions of the hundred-year time-line of the business
cycle, culminating in the Great Depression of 1929-
1939 when seldom less than 10,000,000 employables were
out of work. That is economic war.

Time after time Capital and Labor found it impossible
to arbitrate their differences, so that in any one year there
were several thousand strikes. That is war.

Private, economically powerful citizens overstepped their civil rights and used legislatures, judiciary and executive offices to stamp on liberty. That is war.

Leaders of labor racketeered and sabotaged their own followers . . . fought one another for profit and glory and climbed to personal power on the ruins of rival careers. That is war.

These are but a few exhibits of a culture-wide condition . . . domestic war raging in every industrial nation throughout more years than those of our Great Transition. So intrenched was it on the national home fronts of the earth that in the 1930's not less than 150,-000,000 people lived in poverty—surrounded by technically efficient producing systems. That is war.

The war abroad compelled our engineers to carry factory production to undreamed-of mass, volume, and perfection of straight-line organization, but it did not force them to invent corresponding means of purchasing power. Thus unwittingly the leaders of the war abroad expedited the war at home. The depressions—and the war-tension—became bigger and deeper. The split in the national economic life and the lag of some parts of the culture behind others—specifically the capacity to get goods and services to the people behind the capacity to produce them—grew wider and wider.

So with its tragic destruction and world dislocations, war has brought its positive psychological compensation. By multiplying several-fold the crucial social trends, by separating them sharply from one another, it has permitted the people to see the gaps between them. Thus the war now utters a sharp warning to the people that they must do something about their social-economic problems; it precipitates creative thought and pushes the people to tap hidden reservoirs of power. Our modern Thirty Years War, I say has been nothing less than a generation of clarification—and therefore has served to bring us to a great moment in history.

4.
The Social Flux Is at Free Flow

The fourth imperative lies in the revolutionary nature of our times. We live at the median of the swiftest social transition in all history. The flux of events and mood is at last at free flow. The adamant of a static society has been shaken apart. Changes in social pattern succeed one another so rapidly that the culture is no longer a matrix into which human life is poured, but seems far more like a kaleidoscope. The shifts in western culture are of such dimensions that, if they continue to the year 2000 our great-grandchildren will regard the twentieth century as a Great Transition between two stages of industrial-democratic society.

The first, with its roots in a thousand years of slow change, made its hesitant appearance in the seventeenth century, advanced slowly in the eighteenth, rolled up swiftly in the nineteenth, and came to its close near the turn into our own. The second stage—which may be called the Second Industrial Revolution—was expedited enormously by the 1914-1918 phase of our Thirty Years War and whirled dizzily upward throughout the Long Armistice after 1919 into today's extraordinary crisis in every form of social organization. This is a crisis not merely in the production of things and in political democracy, but in the manners and mores of the entire culture—in the ethics of human relations, in law and morals, in family and marriage, in art and science, in philosophy and religion.

Now is the moment, I say, for the flux is at free flow.

5.

Minds and Moods Have Been Changing

As a consequence, a fifth imperative declares this to be our moment to design a new world: the public mind, long resistant to revolutionary change, has been "softened up." People are ready to listen to the idea that this is a "new day." The social flux, especially the world and domestic upheavals of the Two Wars, has shaken the complacency of hitherto rigid minds. Forty years ago our Victorian leaders were convinced that America was "the best of all possible worlds." But forty years of drastic social change, concluded by ten years of unbroken mass unemployment . . . bread lines . . . public relief . . . ten years of stalled factories and farms and the trial of shockingly novel governmental enterprises—has stirred many of them out of their lethargy and ivory tower assurance. Today, under the impact of undeclared war on civilization, of fascist tyranny, mass murder, and mass torture—"a thousand eyes for an eye" —and the pitiless publicity of print, radio, and film, even our "economic royalists" have given signs of being disturbed in their neo-Victorian cocksureness. Ancient objects of allegiance, long assumed to be permanent, have one by one been discarded. Certainty has given way to doubt, and that in turn to the hesitant beginnings of a new tolerance.

Men's minds and moods have been changing . . . now is the moment for vigorous nation-wide study and public action.

6.

America Discovers New Creative Power

My confidence that now is the moment is bred also of a sixth imperative: we have already entered far into the most creative period in history. Like all the new countries that were born of European culture after the sixteenth century, we have been passing through three stages of creative growth:

First, a long 250-year period of infancy during which our ways of living were imported from the European-British scene.

Second, since 1890 a half century of revolt and improvisation of native statement. Imaginative pioneers on a dozen creative frontiers of the sciences and the arts, social engineering and government have been bursting the bonds of slavish conformity to European and ancient Mediterranean norms, and stating American life as it is really lived. Now in the 1940s we are fifty years beyond the ninth edition of Whitman's *Leaves of Grass*, the first revolutionary buildings of Louis Sullivan, John Dewey's Laboratory School, and Isadora Duncan's "authentic gesture" . . . fifty years of strenuous rebellion against alien forms and a vast cumulation of indigenous power to create an American statement.

As a consequence our social engineers and artists have

been leading American expression beyond revolt and
improvisation into a third period of growth. It is a stage
marked by mature and original design and a thrilling
competence of statement in every creative medium—in
social invention, in the building of the house, in the poem
and the song. The evidence is impressive that this is the
moment to harness the creative power of the country for
the tasks of imaginative design and reconstruction which
lie ahead. Much of this book will document that point.

7.

And we must not overlook a seventh imperative, our
native power is reinforced today by the pick of Europe's
liberal, creative people. For three centuries this historic
Land of Opportunity has lured recurring waves of
pioneering, freedom-loving Europeans: the Puritan Great
Migration of 1629-1640 . . . the waves of west Ger-
mans and Scotch Irish who poured into our ports between 1690 and 1720 . . . the influx of refugee-revolu-
tionaries from the 1830s to the 1850s . . . the Scandi-
navian exodus of the 1870s and 1880s. The latest and
greatest creative Hegira was brought about by Hitler
and Mussolini and the extremes of Russian communism
during the Long Armistice after 1919. A few like Karl
Barth found a sounding board for their Word in Switzer-
land and some embraced nearby England as more con-
genial, but the hardier refugees, 130,000 strong, came to
America. In their forefront is an amazing spearhead of
creative imagination and initiative, including giants in
all the arts and sciences: witness the Einsteins and Manns
. . . such leaders of architecture and industrial design

as Walter Gropius and the Bauhaus group . . . such painters as Georg Grosz and Karl Hofer . . . in the social sciences—the whole School of Exile at the New School of Social Research, and such vigorous creative producers as Pitirim Sorokin at Harvard . . . in psychology and education—the renowned leaders of the Gestalt School: Max Wertheimer, Wolfgang Koehler, and the late Kurt Koffka—and many others. But we need not multiply names to illustrate that Europe's creative loss is our spectacular gain.

DANGER SIGNALS IN THE SOCIAL TRENDS THEMSELVES

Ten years ago under the compelling revelation of the stalling of the world's production plants I sent you some lines:

> When in the calculus of human events
> The curves of interdependent social trends
> either pass points of inflection
> or produce equations of different orders
> Men of intelligence revise their systems of thought
> and design new courses of democratic action.

8.

The Curve of Culture Has Passed Points of Inflection

The eighth imperative—and I mean imperative—that now is the moment to do something about our social order—is that the curves of social trend have passed "points of inflection" and that we must revise our ideas accordingly and design new machinery to fit the new conditions. If we fail to do that, the social-economic system will continue to stall and eventually break down.

Under the impact of the new facts piled up by the Great Depression (1929-1939), three distinguished groups of scholars, recognizing the necessity for social-economic reconstruction, buckled down to the difficult task of making a complete and objective appraisal of the social system. Professional economists, sociologists, and engineers turned from mechanical to social problems of engineering,[1] boldly sought to discover:

—how the really foundational trends of the social system were moving . . .
—what the relation of the acceleration of one was to that of the others . . .
—how much the American people could produce with the existing economic structure . . .
—how much they could consume . . .
—why their purchasing power lagged so sharply behind their productive capacity . . .
—and a tentative answer to the most profound question of all: "What is holding us back?"

[1] Conspicuous among the published documents were the research monographs of one of America's most distinguished engineers and mathematical analysts—Bassett Jones: *Debt and Production* and his *Horses and Apples* (John Day Company, 1933); the volumes of the world-renowned economists of the Brookings Institution in Washington: Harold G. Moulton, *et al., America's Capacity to Produce; America's Capacity to Consume* (Brookings Institution, Washington, D. C., 1934); and the engineers' studies: Harold Loeb, *et al., The Chart of Plenty* (Viking Press, 1935), and the *Report of the National Survey of Potential Produce Capacity* (The New York City Housing Authority and the Works Division of the Emergency Relief Bureau, City of New York, 1935). Meanwhile the National Resources Committee (now the National Resources Planning Board) published the first of its epoch-marking *Technological Trends and National Policy, Problems of a Changing Population,* and others. In 1933 I published my own analysis of the total problem and of the grave necessity of nation-wide adult education concerning it in *The Great Technology: Social Chaos and the Public Mind* (John Day Company).

This new quantitative study of the productive capacity sprang out of and rounded out a full generation of statistical analysis of other parts of the social order. As the entire system stalled in the Great Depression the nation's scholars assembled, organized and analyzed this vast mass of quantitative data concerning practically every phase of social life. From the experience of a generation of research in fitting curves to the historical data of rates of population-growth and, especially, from Mr. Bassett Jones' epoch-marking work in making a metrical analysis of the time-quantity relations between the measurable facts of a hundred years of economic production, they knew that the curves of social trends were dangerously out of step and that our national productive system *could* produce much more than it had ever succeeded in doing. And they had pretty good appraisals of what was holding us back.

One conclusion of major importance emerges from these quantitative studies:

> *Our times—especially the fifteen years from 1905 to 1920—constitutes the "critical" period in the first long stage of industrialism. The plotted curves of rate of growth in population, in the production of metals and alloys, fuels, fibers, foods, of basic commodities, in literacy and other social phenomena—change from positive to negative in our period. This is clear proof of the transitional nature of our times.*

This generalization rivets tight the conclusion from the other assembled evidence and logic, and forces me to conclude that now is the moment in which we not only can but must take the social system in hand and redirect its course. The plotted curves of the rate of growth of the social system illustrate the evidence that our years constitute a true mathematical "point of inflection"[2] on the curve of western culture. Such points, attention-centering phenomena to any mathematician, are, when located on curves of social trend, clear danger signals to a people. They tell us with fidelity when our economic-political-psychological theories as well as our social practices must be looked into; when, indeed, we not only can but must reconstruct certain parts of our social system.

9.

The Interdependent Curves of Social Trend Are of Different Orders

The ninth imperative is coordinate with the eighth—it is that the equations of crucial constituent curves are of markedly different orders. Some have exponents of only 2 . . . some of 3, 4, 5 . . . some even of 8, 9, or 10. This means that some parts of the culture lag far behind—dangerously behind—other parts of the culture. These findings document mathematically Professor William Ogburn's much-discussed generalization of "culture

[2] Points of inflection on growth curves are points at which the *rate* of growth changes from "positive" to "negative." Note, for example, that curves which portray the history of the rate of growth of such social phenomena as population, production of basic commodities, illiteracy, and the like rise more rapidly with each advancing year or decade—until our own day. This is called "positive acceleration." Then between 1905 and 1920 the shape of each of these curves shifts, flattens out, and gradually approaches a horizontal. The *rate* of growth has slowed down; this is called "negative acceleration." If this is continued far enough the point at which the curve flattens out, shifts from positive to negative acceleration, is called a point of inflection. It is "critical" because it marks a real shift in the rate of growth.

lag," stated twenty years ago. I am impelled to quote
some more of those lines I sent you ten years ago.

Out of the dawn of the new industrial culture
Three Curves of interdependent social trends
Traced themselves on the moving record of history
Economic Productivity . . . Social Invention . . . Popular
     Consent.

Throughout the first Day of Industrialism
It was taken for granted that all three would rise
Sufficiently synchronized to preserve social stability
But under the momentum of expansion
Economic productivity was sharply accelerated
While social invention and popular consent
Lagged cumulatively behind.

                    .   .   .

Meanwhile other constituent trends, such as the growth of
     population,
Which had given birth to the advance of man's produc-
     tivity,
   Passed points of inflection
And gave fair warning of impending social change.

I give a single example from the scholars' studies—the
lag of population behind both production and productivity. Bear in mind that during the latter half of the
nineteenth century population and the production of all
basic commodities grew with accelerating crescendo. It
was a period of tremendous expansion, motivated by the
idea of *More!* More people to buy more shoes, hats, suits,
houses, food. More power stations, more factories, more
cars, more goods to export to "backward" populations.
More of everything. The swift building of the industrial
structure and the expansion of the population—most of

the people young enough to be within the effective age-range of occupational efficiency . . . few needing care at public expense—contributed to keep the system going without the necessities of careful design. The depressions that came every decade were pretty bad, but not so violent as to stall the system entirely. Then during the first episode (1914-1918) of the Thirty Years War came the enormous speeding up of the economic system, and at the same time a sharp slowing down of population growth.

The equations of Mr. Bassett Jones' curves show very significantly that the rate of population growth lagged behind the rate at which the productivity of a worker in mechanized industry advanced. That is, specifically, while the rate of population growth was advancing as "the square of the time," that of production was growing as "the cube of the time" (of some commodities as the 4th, 5th, 6th power of the time) and—most significant of all for the problem of unemployment in a technically efficient civilization—the productivity of a worker was multiplying faster than most other social phenomena, namely as the 4th power of the time.[3]

These brief examples from the scholars' researches illustrate what I mean when I say that we now know quite exactly that our years are the critical ones on the curve of western culture in which the lag has become so great that we have to do something about consciously redesigning the social system. Thus far, it has "just

---

[3] Stated in equational form:

Population	$Pop = kt^2$
Production	$Prod = kt^3$
Productivity	$Man\ Hours = kt^{-4}$

growed," creaking and stalling seriously. The technical efficiency of the production of quantity goods mounted, new industries appeared, but intermittent mass-unemployment remained the characteristic condition. Today, the dangerous lags of distribution (what I call "social invention," including government) behind production have become so great that the social system has to be taken in hand, redesigned and rebuilt in many places, if it is to be kept going efficiently.

But that means that new concepts must be found to replace the old outmoded ones and that new social machinery has to be invented to fit them. For example, as the rate of population growth slowed down, became stationary, the average length of life of the American people increased to beyond 65 . . . the advancing requirements of technical skill and energy on the worker dropped the "old age dead line" in industry from 65 to 40, and the proportion of the population to be supported by public taxation increased swiftly. It was clear that the old ideas—namely, that the American worker was young and vigorous and that there would always be work for all in American industry—were no longer true.

✓   ✓   ✓

Similarly, concepts of "expanding economy," scarcity, *laissez-faire*, "law of supply and demand"—basic to the nineteenth century economists—began to take on a new meaning or to be out-moded! For example, "an expanding economy" came to mean—not of more people, but of more life—a far richer way of living which could be got by running the social system at its maximum and distributing the life obtained to the people.

The old idea that physical things were really scarce

was outmoded by such findings as the Brookings statement that the standard of life need not be less than 3000
to 3500 (1929) dollars per family per year and the engineers' estimate of a potential national income of nearly
$120,000,000,000. There was a storm of dissent from the
Center-to-Right and much shouting of bad names at
these students of the social system. But the second great
episode, 1939   , of the Thirty Years War has given
an awe-inspiring hint of what our production actually
can be; we know beyond a doubt that the engineers were
right, that now so far as the producing system is concerned we can have abundance.

The Jones analysis also augmented the questioning of
other long-accepted ideas—one of the most important
being the concept of *laissez-faire*. The sum total of the
advancing social trends had increased the conviction that
laissez-faire was outmoded, and by fifty years of legislation our statesmen revealed their acceptance of that idea,
redefining "freedom" as "designed control" rather than
"absence of restraint." Thus the very definition of the
central concept of democracy—freedom—came in for
an increasing amount of criticism and re-interpretation.

As new ideas slowly ousted old ones the whole problem of "purchasing power," including the respective
share of owners, managers, and workers in the national
income, was subjected to critical review. It was formerly
assumed that there was a definite discoverable relation—
established on a basis of bargaining between owners and
workers—of what a worker could produce to what society could pay him for it. However, concepts have
changed steadily and at the present transitional moment,
there seems to be no discernible relation on such a bar-

gaining basis between what a worker in quantity production industries can produce and what society can
pay him for producing it.

10.

Now . . . or Never!

The most critical point I have saved for last. It's negative. It's frightening. I hope it will be compelling enough
to make us act:

> This is our moment, now in the 1940s,
> Because . . . there won't be another—in our Day.

I can't prove it in a paragraph; in the remainder of
this little book I shall try to present the evidence and
the argument. Here I can merely quote the judgment of
social engineers in and out of government—namely,
that if our people turn their backs on a sick world, if we
refuse to run our economic system full tilt, the engine
of our domestic system will stall worse than ever before
. . . and eventually break down altogether.

The alternative will be a fascist managed society.

"I Tell the Signs of the Answerer."

Rollo Brown tells you in his beautiful little book that
   "There must be a new song."
I say to you the new song is being sung . . .
The greatest poems are being written . . .
The singers are coming to life . . .
The Answerers are speaking.

The American is the maker of poems,
   The Answerer.
What can be answered . . . he answers.

America is Answerers.

Two

THE AMERICAN CULTIVATES
HIS VALLEY

Let me tell you a story.

A PEOPLE CAME INTO A VALLEY

Over the mountains they came, on foot, in wagons, on horses . . . without machines. They looked down on a land of unexampled virgin nourishment for man, his plants, his animals. They looked down on a land of beauty and variety—rich forested mountains and green-grassed valleys for the taking and sustaining . . . out-cropping deposits of stone to be quarried, clay to be made into bricks . . . coal, iron, copper, phosphorus to be mined and manufactured, and gigantic potential power on the steep running streams to be dammed. Here in one giant river basin—it was a single unique watershed—were the makings of an admirable cultivated scene.

> Something there is in a man . . .
> Distrusts the deferred security of Tomorrow

These colonial cultivators of the land and house, trailing the western sun, cut the clearings for the first temporary shelters, stumped the fields and planted their farms.

First comers got the rich bottom lands along the streams and turned nomad shelter into civilized habitation. Some, more sensitive to organic problems of life on the land, turned temporary plantings into diversified, sustained-yield farms, and in the next generation transformed shelter and habitation into architecture—functional and indigenous. Late comers and those less thoughtful and patient threw up their rough habitations in the canyons of the hills and grubbed a meager sustenance out of steep slopes and thin anemic soil. Still others, more ambitious and shrewd concerning the money, the power, and the glory, became the middle-men between producers and staked out the strategic river and land portages at the crossroads of inevitable trade and built and bossed the manufacturing and market towns.

Generation succeeded generation until six had passed. From mountain tops the men of the sixth generation could look down upon a civilization which from not-too-near views looked good—corn farms, cotton farms, fruit farms, hundreds of little villages, here and there a manu-facturing city, coal mines, iron mines, copper mines, phosphate mines, fertilizer plants, and occasional power stations at little dams across the rivers.

The years passed. The families that grew up in the Valley, over-appraising the power of renewal that lay in the land, over-planted it with annual recurrences of crops . . . over-cut the trees, neglecting to plant in pro-portion to the cutting . . . over-mined the fuels, metals, and fertilizers . . . and under-estimated the water that dropped from heaven into that marvelous watershed. There was little conscious waste—if one excepts the ab-sentee-owned lumber companies that came in the fifth generation and ruthlessly denuded the hills for immediate profit. Yet—not enough of the people knew the great principle of permanent civilization building—the Principle of the Sustained Yield. It was an ancient concept but only a few farmers of the Valley and their science-trained sons in the university experiment stations understood it and lived by it. It simply was that for life in the Valley to continue generation after generation, and to be good, all the kinds of soil in the culture must be nourished . . . "Put back into the land," it said, "and so into the people, as much as you take out." This was the principle of the sustained yield, simple and long known . . . but the inertia of the people was too great to think it and practice it.

So the rains came—fifty inches a year; six thousand tons of water fell each year on each acre of that Valley. And the floods came. There were the floods-you-see, the torrents of the streams pouring their tribute into the great River each spring, destroying low land farms and causing annual disaster in populous cities. And there were the floods-you-don't-see; billions of invisible streamlets gnawing their way through the topsoil of the farms, carrying away the precious chemical foods for plant growth down to the streams, for the great River to push them two thousand miles to the Sea below and build them up into the richest Delta land on man's earth.

Generation succeeded generation until six had passed. Then with almost indiscernible increments the people of the Valley slowly recognized that instead of sustaining the yield they had spent their magnificent inheritance. Much was heard at the crossroads and in the meetings about—Erosion! "To gnaw away," it meant . . . a dramatic word to make conscious to a people how they had done again what their ancestors in all places and at all times had done before them: slaughtered their forests . . . exposed the heavy ground cover of vegetation . . . gnawed away the corn patches and the cotton fields and the vegetable plots. The soil was eroded too, the precious top soil, a million years in the making, gnawed away in a generation, never to be replaced in this epoch of man's life on earth.

The erosion did not spare the people; witness: the soil thins, plant foods disappear, crops become anemic, cash income declines, diet weakens, energy subsides, the people lose courage and enthusiasm, the children are undernourished and undertaught. This is the erosion of the people.

✓ ✓ ✓

But the Country which held that great Valley within it was composed of eleven Valleys like it and each one subdivided into lesser constituent ones. Through these other great Valleys the people had lived during six . . . yes— seven, eight, and even nine generations and had cultivated their scenes. They too gnawed away their land, wore down their industries and only in rare instances did they sustain the yield. Steadily the capital plant took nourishment away from consumer goods and purchasing power. Owner took too much . . . worker got too little. As that happened the distribution system also eroded . . . slowed down the production facilities. Time after time in those eleven great Valleys the producing mechanisms refused to work because sustaining purchasing power did not flow back into it. Industrial erosion!

And one day in the tenth generation of the oldest of

those Valleys it seemed that the whole continental mechanism stood stalled. Outside the factories of a thousand cities skilled men, eager to work, looked dumbly at their idle machines. Beside six million farms the agrarians stood with foodstuffs for those idle urban men. And there was no means of keeping the goods and the foods in transit. From metropolitan financial centers agencies of communication and buying and selling reached into every market place of the earth; but they were silent.

Then the leaders in the capital city of the eleven Valleys and the students in the university centers of self-cultivation knew that the moment had come when the Exploitive Tradition had run its course. They knew that now the thinking men must take thought to rebuild the land, to reprime the factories and the banks, to renourish the markets, and to put purchasing power into the hands of the troubled people . . . if—it was not too late.

> Out of the devastating experience of immediate profit-taking Man came to prize the deferred security of tomorrow.

THE PEOPLE UP-BUILD THE VALLEY—SUSTAIN THE YIELD

Throughout the last of the six generations, as the people vaguely sensed that things were not right with them, timorous steps had been taken to try to stop the erosion and to repair the effects of the wind and weather. Under several administrations at the Capital conservational movements had been launched, and in parts of the Valley itself local attempts were made to remedy the injured farms and crippled cities. Engineers knew that the

nub of reconstruction was to control the River, for the
Valley was a single watershed from which the fifty inches
of rain a year drained too quickly through the River.
But all local attempts around the rim of that watershed
were abortive, partly because there was no single sovereignty over the land. In the generations of settlement the
law of natural priority and preëmption had usurped the
role of intelligent social design and had divided that
organic region which the watershed created among
seven arbitrarily apportioned "state governments." These
were unwilling, perhaps unable, to find the mood and the
money—for this was a pecuniary civilization—necessary
to harness the great River.

And then the thing happened.

The governing leaders of the Country came into that
Valley. They brought the single federal sovereignty over
all the seven quarreling parts needed to stir inert life. Because of this sovereignty they could help the people in
two other ways—divert money from other and richer
Valleys to this needy one . . . and bring to the latter
from the richest cultural centers of the nation the scientific and engineering knowledge and the coöperative experience so badly needed.

A single national Authority was created—a Federal
"government yardstick corporation" with vast financial
resources, and an assembly of true social engineers fore-
gathered. These social engineers were artists as well as
technologists; they were "orderers"; they could think and
design regionally. No provincialism or partisanship of
state, or party, or community governed their minds.
Trained to design before they built, they saw the Valley
as a single unitary watershed. They saw it as a potential

organization, exploited by thoughtless men, needing order more than all else. The watershed . . . the River
. . . must be controlled—as a unit, they said.

Naturally, the thing happened. An example of the
scientific and democratic way of doing things came to
life on that land such as man had never seen before. It
seemed that surely a stride toward the instatement of the
Great Tradition on the continent was being taken. It was
premonitory of the coming moment when social life in
all the eleven Valleys could be made good for men. And
we must see it that way—as what happens when a people
parallel private initiative with the social enterprise of the
government yardstick corporation, producing actually a
great popular cultural yardstick—a precipitant of a new
national life.

✦ ✦ ✦

What they did in less than a decade is now a matter of
voluminous record: fourteen powerful dams . . . a
made-to-order lake—a vast inland water system—640
miles long . . . giant power radiating out of that Valley
to light and heat and power the towns and homes and
factories in nineteen states—at two cents a kilowatt hour
—where four cents had been the rate only five years before . . . The dams controlled the River and the water
on the watershed, and the floods-you-see in one vast centralized engineering project. The giant reservoirs held
back the upstream waters in the wet seasons and released
them in the dry ones, preventing the annual overflow of a
million farms and scores of cities.

Some there were who feared centralization . . . "It
means dictatorship," they warned; "beware of standardization. If Government helps, it will control." But those

social engineers were of the Great Tradition and they were Americans. The Exploitive Tradition has had its day, they said, and now the true American Way—"I'll do this and you'll do that" . . . "I and We, doing it together" shall be tried. And it did come about in that Valley—a fine fusion of centralization of sovereignty and financing, design and total administration, hand in hand with a decentralized ownership and a "grass-roots" operation. Both federal and local authorities they said, should take part—the federal government doing the things for which it was best equipped, the state and local government doing others, and the private companies, the co-operative associations and individuals doing still others. "Each singing what belongs to him, or to her, and to none else." And so it worked out.

In a thousand crossroad hamlets farmers found their neighbors and discovered a new security. Using the designs and methods of the federal engineers, led by their own county agents, these men of the soil built a great system of experimental farms. In the war on erosion the collaboration of federal engineers designing plans, state and county agents setting them up on the farms of the Valley, the farmers—long from book learning—studying as they worked and working as they studied, conserved their soil. They built check dams and filled in the horrible gullied gashes in the fields. They planted clover, lespedeza, alfalfa, and other legumes. They created pastures and renewed woodlands to restore the soil; built terraces and strip-cropped and plowed on the contour to hold the water on hilly land.

But, controlling the River and distributing to the

people the profits of that control was only a small part of what those social engineers did. At the great dams the federal plants manufactured new phosphorus fertilizers which now went via the coöperatives and the county agents onto the anemic soil of the farm. New farm machines and implements designed by federal engineers, manufactured by private "free" enterprises, and sold at a profit and at a price within the farmers' pocketbooks: electric hay dryers, hillside seeders, threshers, feed grinders, harvesting attachments, rural refrigerators, to preserve perishable farm products almost from the moment they are picked until they are sold in distant cities. In June of one year there were only one thousand cooperating demonstration farms in the Valley; in September four years later there were twenty-six thousand.

So the great war on erosion went on . . . the Exploitive Tradition was set back . . . the Great Tradition got its chance. The people of the Valley rebuilt their farms, their towns, their industries and their transportation, their public health, education, parks, and playgrounds. From being man the Exploiter, the flood maker, the desert maker, having violated the sustained yield principle, the American in the Valley learned to put back into the culture the equivalent of the nourishment taken out.

ย ย ย

The astonishing by-product in esthetics has been not the least of the thrilling as well as the unexpected outcomes: In the very doing of these things of social utility the Americans up-building in the Valley have at the same moment been creating original and indigenous art.

The very process of creating an efficient thing—like a designed dam, a bridge, a generator, a powerhouse—produced an organization—and hence a thing of beauty.

Moreover, this collaboration of architects, farmers, engineers, business men, scientists, builders has generated a larger social view of architecture; man working upon the whole of his environment to put it into habitable, workable, agreeable, and friendly shape. These new social products are things, as Talbot Hamlin says, "that all of us can understand, things built for our own use, buildings made to give us greater power, greater happiness, greater richness of life." As the commemorative plaques on all the dams and powerhouses say, these were "Built for the People of the United States," and one editor adds, not only "for" but "by" the people of the United States, for these are social ventures. But by the collaboration of designers great works of art were brought forth. The Director of New York City's Museum of Modern Art, in opening the TVA photographic show, said that these new dams, powerhouses and other buildings now rank as about "the greatest architecture that America has produced."

And so, America speaks!

In once-dying valleys come alive again
　　with prosperous farms and towns,
In once dread dust plains now green again,
And once cut-over woodless mountains now forested—

　　She speaks!

✓　✓　✓

The story of civilization has always been the story of man cultivating the Valley. In the Nile and the Fertile

Crescent it was so . . . in the Yellow and the Indus-
Ganges . . . in the Danube. Today in the Mississippi
and its continental tributaries . . . in the Connecticut
and its housing of the New Englander . . . in the
Colorado and the man-made gardens of the nature-made
deserts . . . in all the eleven great Valleys of our America. Here on our continent is a whole new cultivation of
the Valley, through the coöperative work of social engineers, regional geographers and sociologists, architects
and industrial designers, statesmen, artists, and teachers
who are dramatically making over the lives of millions of
the people. In every medium the Great Tradition is beginning to be instated on a large scale, aggrandizing Individuals are being sublimated into coöperative Persons.
Walt Whitman's "multitudes of individuals" . . . his
"En Masse" . . . Democracy in the large are coming
alive in divers ways: in vast regional reconstruction . . .
in the rejuvenation of the Great Plains stretching over
eleven states . . . in the cultivation of the Inland Empire of the Columbia River Valley.

But we must see this new up-building of the Great
Tradition on the American land in a more intimate, more
personal way as well, and that is most effectively illustrated by the emergence of the New House of the American.

THE NEW HOUSE OF THE AMERICAN

Yes, America speaks through a new House.
In the pure architecture of her streamlined skyscrapers,
    dams, and powerhouses . . .
In the landscape-fitted lines of her new family houses,
In their interior designs and in the planned communities.

I mean House in the broad, deep sense of the great Master Architects—Louis Henry Sullivan and Frank Lloyd Wright and the industrial and community designers. I mean in the sense of the total cultivation of the American scene—man living and building integrally, organically on the land.

Let me tell you another story.

A MAN CULTIVATES A SCENE

Into the Valley comes a Man. To a naked plateau on unlived-on mountainside he comes to work, to produce, to have a family, to build his House. He does part of what he came to do. He settles on his mountain land, just below the plateau. He puts up mere shelter that serves him as habitation against the ravages of wind and weather. Slowly he builds his competence. His family grows. In many ways he makes his statement, satisfying in part his advancing growth, but leaving much unsaid.

Then . . . he knows. He must build his House. On the plateau it shall be, looking across his farm neighbors' cultivation of the little valley below, presided over by a dozen wooded mountains. His own unique House . . . "what belongs to him and to none else" . . . appropriate to the life that he aspires to be lived there. Not shelter, nor even habitation would he build—but architecture. A House appropriate to the terrain and landscape of the wild mountain forest . . . appropriate to the geography of the Valley and to the aggregation of Valleys . . . appropriate to the expressional culture which his years with the native craftsmen and sophisticated artists—both true creatives—had made him feel.

So he builds his House and cultivates his scene—a room at a time . . . whenever he has grown to another room.

A house indigenous to the land and the local culture; built by local labor from the stone, sand, and gravel of the Man's own hillside . . . property-dividing walls torn down, the field rock brought to the plateau, lovingly appraised and chosen stone by stone . . . the local soils and native trees, birches—white and black, maples, oaks, moved onto the gravelly rock plateau and sheltering foliage nursed around the expanding House. Like his mentor, Louis Sullivan, "necessity, not tradition" compels every increment of design and construction; the necessity the Man felt organically by the slow accretion of living on the land. Out of no worship of either familiar or classic styles, but out of long months of looking and absorbing, come sensitized intuitions . . . organic awareness of true functionality, in terms of the needs of life . . . and of these he builds.

The ever-present task, before he builds and step by step as he builds, is design—form imagined, to fit the needs of the life to be lived there. But if the design of the man's House is to be truly organic—not to be merely a mosaic, of isolated and non-functioning bits—one organism, the owner-designer, must experience it—for only he can be truly sensitive to the life to be lived in it. One "architect"—himself serving as integrator of the ideas and feelings of engineer, interior designer, landscaper, psychologist, sociologist, philosopher—must gather technical assistance from a great many sources and organize those into a unified product. This concept, repeatedly stated by Frank Lloyd Wright and the moderns, is comparable to Gordon Craig's idea that the theatre can become organic only as a *"regisseur"*—an artist-director—draws together the processes of writer, actor, stage designer,

scene painter, architect, musician, costume designer, and
the others.

✓　✓　✓

Thus the Man builds his house and through it helps to
build a new conception of the House of the American.
Not a mere building of sticks and stones, but a harmoni-
ous fusion of the land, the site, the setting in community,
valley, region, nation, and country . . . the approaches
to these and the conditions and trends of population, new
materials, new power, new transport and communication,
new "housing" finance for families hitherto deprived of
their proper houses because of society's failure to solve
the "money" problem. In brief: the House of the American is interpreted as his total cultivated scene.

Multiply the Man and his House a thousand times?
You have a community cultivating its scene. Multiply
him a million times? A hundred million? You have a
people cultivating the American scene.

"The Signs of the Answerer"

Two stories I have told you. Each is true. Each is a
sign of the Answerer.

> I say to you a new song is being sung—
> The greatest poems are being written—
> The American is the maker of poems.
> The Answerer.

What can be answered he answers—in whole designed
valleys . . . in the attractive houses, spacious lawns
and gardens and parks of the federal government's
Greenbelt communities . . . in the made-to-order vil-

lage—Norris, Tennessee . . . in Chicago's slum clearance Jane Addams Houses and Trumbull Park homes . . . in Santa Rita—planned city development near Austin, Texas . . . in the new camps for migratory workers in California . . . in a current spectacular example of prefabrication now solving one of Defense Housing's problems—namely, Buckminster Fuller's Dymaxion House—circular, all-metal, assembled by six man-days of unskilled labor, accommodating a family of five—cost, including furniture—$1200 . . . in the defense housing of George Howe and company—prefabricated, economical, functional houses, average cost $3500, using glass and openness of design to let in sun, grouped around open lawns, "partitioned to privacy by walled-in porches."

Two "Answerers" of the House

As I have been documenting my thesis that this is our moment I have been thinking much about two of America's true Answerers—Louis Henry Sullivan (1856-1924) and Frank Lloyd Wright (1869-   ). By their buildings as well as by their words these two frontiersmen of American creative life have proved my thesis that man can, by thinking and feeling great original and moving ideas, actually redivert social trend, even start whole populations off on new ones. For they actually did it! Sullivan, since 1880, and Wright, since 1900, successfully led a revolt against the worship of classic alien forms of expression. They imagined new concepts of American culture and new designs appropriate to them. They built these in more than a hundred buildings each. And they made their philosophy of the House of the American articulate in words. Sullivan was the trail-blazer and leader of the revolt and improvisation. Wright, a student of Sullivan, carried on the pioneering but has lived to see his own work move American architecture into our own stage of mature organic expression.

The story of the fight of the artists Sullivan and Wright against the merchandiser-builders—Daniel H. Burnham and his associates, for example—is a fight between the Producer and the Middleman . . . between Democratic power and Feudal power . . . indeed it is the age-long struggle of the Great Tradition against the Exploitive Tradition, about which much of my book is written.

Of the two rival traditions as exemplified in American building, Sullivan said:

Thus, there came into prominence in the architectural world of Chicago two firms, Burnham & Root and Adler & Sullivan. In each firm was a man with a fixed irrevocable purpose in life, for the sake of which he would bend or sacrifice all else. Daniel Burnham was obsessed by the feudal idea of power. Louis Sullivan was equally obsessed by the beneficent idea of Democratic power. Daniel chose the easier way, Louis the harder.[1]

For years Sullivan almost alone not only built indigenously, organically; but led the denunciation of nation-wide imitation of British-classical styles in building.

Thus we have now the abounding freedom of Eclecticism, the winning smile of taste, but no architecture. For Architecture, be it known, is dead . . . There is now a dazzling display of merchandise, all imported, excepting to be sure our own cherished colonial, which maintains our Anglo-Saxon tradition in its purity. We have Tudor for colleges

[1] Louis Sullivan, *Autobiography of an Idea*, p. 288.

and residences; Roman for banks, and railway stations, and libraries—or Greek if you like—some customers prefer the Ionic to the Doric. We have French, English and Italian Gothic, Classic and Renaissance for Churches. In fact we are prepared to satisfy, in any manner of taste. Residences we offer in Italian or Louis Quinze. We make a small charge for alterations and adaptations. Our service we guarantee as exceptional and exclusive. Our importations are direct. We have our own agents abroad.[2]

Sullivan, himself an integration of technically competent engineer and sensitive artist, proved to be the first to see clearly that a building must be organic, expressing the mood, rhythm, and philosophy of the culture as well as be definitely appropriate to the life that is to be lived in it. Just before he died he stated the principle and the concepts of its practical achievement in his *Autobiography of an Idea*. The "Idea," "function determines form," is the product of a lifetime of search, design, and building, and has now become even the shibboleth of the schools. Of every member of a building—and equally of every word in a poem or prose page, of every gesture of the body, of every activity of the new school—Louis Sullivan taught us all to ask: What is this thing to do? What is the function of this part? What is this beam or column to hold up? What shade of meaning is this phrase to convey? What mood is this gesture to evoke? What attitudes and ideas is this activity to develop? Of each one he asks: Does this have a function? Is it needed? Is it indispensable? Can I find something better?

During the 1890s Mr. Wright was with his "Lieber Meister" for six years. Since then he has designed and

[2] *Ibid.*, p. 325-326.

constructed over a hundred buildings around the world, including some that are recognized masterpieces of architecture; for example: Taliesin, his own Homestead, Workshop, and School . . . "Teikoku," the Imperial Hotel—of all the public buildings it alone was left standing when the 1923 earthquake razed Tokyo . . . the Johnson Building, Racine, Wisconsin, exciting experiment in the design of a house of business . . . and the Kaufman "Falling Water" in Pennsylvania, an equally thrilling success in the building of a country house.

Like his great teacher, Mr. Wright is an integrator of the culture. In poetic feeling, scientific knowledge and practical experience, he *is* the fusion of traits he sees in the culture—engineer, practicing architect and creative artist. He, too, refused the rule of commercialism, and megaphoned Sullivan's blasts at our Europeanized eclecticism. Year after year he denounced the "borrowed finery" of the "plan factories" of the cheap architects— "sartorial artists"—who gave the "vulgar rich" what they wanted. Can't you hear him telling Chicago in 1902 that the realtor who predicted that, when Chicago "got after culture, she'd make culture hum!" was a sound prophet. Well, she had and did! What "cultured" America wanted, and got, was the best styles of all the ages in one grandiose mosaic—a fearfully and wonderfully made house, with a Greek front porch, Roman dome and arches, oriental turrets and towers, even a bit of our own "pure colonial"—and all in the mood of being "somewhat" Gothic.

For his vigorous sweeping of alien forms of building from the American scene Mr. Wright long paid the penalty of isolation from the bulk of his profession.

Gradually, however, the revolt against the grip of alien and classical styles and the improvisation of American forms of expression advanced in every medium: in letters and thence through the work of a whole new school of poets, novelists and playwrights . . . in the dance under Isadora Duncan's tremendous impetus . . . in philosophy through Peirce, James, Dewey, and the pragmatists, and Santayana, Royce, and the poets . . . in the graphic and plastic arts through a score of leaders inspired by such adamant personalities as Alfred Stieglitz . . . in the critical study of the social order by Veblen, Turner, Thomas, Boas, and the New Historians.

✶ ✶ ✶

Frank Lloyd Wright on Architecture,[3] the cumulative statement of Wright's philosophy of Man living well on the land, shows that he has made himself Master among American architects primarily because he has constantly applied his energies to the study of Man and his changing cultures. To him the land is primary architecture and Man must take his cue from that. The House is the revealing expression of the total culture. The life of integrity, he insists, is "growth becoming the law of the land"—families living on the land, communities living on the land, nations living on the land.

Perhaps Wright's best statement of the outcome of a life of total cultivation of the scene is his vision of the future community of the American, which he calls "Broadacre City." The central concept in cultural reconstruction, as revealed in the models of the community itself, is decentralization: little farms . . . little homes

---

[3] A conspicuous event in the publishing world was the issuing in the winter of 1941-42 of this book edited by Frederick Gutheim.

. . . little factories . . . little universities . . . little laboratories for professional men. The imagined community is a "county seat" town of 1400 families . . . four square miles of typical countryside in the temperate zone . . . five acres per family. Here is a community design of diversified houses, as diverse as the owners and their incomes, their personalities, and their varied lives, all harmoniously integrated into one fabric.

Sullivan's great principle matures in Wright's Broadacre design and building.

Form and function are one . . . The emphasis has been placed upon diversity and unity . . . every kind of builder would be likely to have a jealous eye to the harmony of the whole within broad limits fixed by the county architect . . . each county would thus naturally develop an individuality of his own . . . Architecture in the broad sense of the term would thrive naturally.

In the houses there is no distinction in quality. "Quality is in all, for all, alike . . . The difference is only in individuality and extent. There is nothing poor or mean anywhere in Broadacres."

He has no illusions that we will instate Broadacre City on the land next year. "We will probably witness no sudden change;" but "we already see the acceleration that precedes decay, and we see the machine power which overbuilt the present city, at work tearing it down." Nothing can hold it together, "except the cupidity that exploits current stupidities . . . The city has become the overcrowded crowd. Too many lives piled upon one another become obstructive to life . . . The remedy lies within the causes of such destruction . . . We die so that life may live in greater abundance."

Thus a country of farms and "small towns" is visualized, tied together by an efficient, safe and beautiful architecture of transport and communication—monorail railways, twelve-lane arterial highways (for every Broadacre citizen has one or more motor cars), no grade crossings, no left turns, no visible signals, lamp posts, ditches, curbs . . . 200-miles-an-hour family Aerotors replace the aeroplane. Three inventions are already building Broadacres: the motor car, electrical intercommunication, standardized machine-shop production.

↗ ↗ ↗

The philosophic roots of this new vision and design are those of the Great Tradition of the Individual, expressed as a "new freedom for living in America" . . . based on his conception of the "just rights of man" . . . "freedom to decentralize, redistribute and correlate the properties of the work of man on earth to his birth right, which is the ground itself." Wright also makes his statement of the three inherent social rights of man, which must be guaranteed through popular government: "(1) His social right to a simple direct medium of exchange in place of gold as commodity: some form of universal social credit. (2) His social right to his place on the ground as he has had his right to the sun and air: land to be held only by use and improvements. (3) His social right to the ideas by which and for which he lives: that is to say public ownership of invention and scientific discoveries that concern the life of the people." Here, I say is the Great Tradition's positive definition of the freedoms and of property;[4] a ringing denial of the validity of the Exploitive Tradition's "absence of restraint" defini-

[4] See Chapters III and IV for the development of this idea.

tion of freedom and the creative, preëmptive withholding-from-use concept of property.

Government in a Broadacres civilization, in order to be
democratic, must be "little" also . . . of the people, by
the people, and for people . . . decentralized. Yet it is
centralized also, because "all public utilities are concentrated in the hands of the state and the various county
governments, as are also matters of administration, patrol,
fire, post, banking, license, and record, thus making politics a vital matter to everyone in the new city instead of
the present hopeless indifference that makes 'politics' a
grafter's profession."

Some of the free-enterprisers and their politicians
shouted "socialism"; others, "state capitalism"; still others
weren't sure whether it was perhaps "fascism"! when
Wright first made his proposal. Yet, he says, it is really
"organic capitalism" . . . "broadly and firmly based
upon the ground . . . Individuality established" in private ownership of productive and residence land and the
buildings upon it. Moreover, the forms of genuine democratic life, personally designed, flexible and shifting are
free plastic forms and freedom is "about the last thing a
socialized state would care to encounter or try to conquer. The very solidarity of a true democratic success
would terrorize them more than their planes and guns
would terrorize us."

Unemployment and all its evils are ended forever.
"There would never be labor enough, nor could there be
under-consumption. Whatever a man did would be well
done . . . because done mostly by himself in his own interest, under the most valuable inspiration and direction
. . . Economic independence would be near every man

who worked; a subsistence certain, a life varied and interesting is the inevitable consequence. Nothing too good
for anybody—and no substitute sought for quality."

✓ ✓ ✓

I have told you two stories . . . true stories . . . and
shown you Two Answerers at work leading the people
in building a better America. These men of design feel
the American land and the life that is being lived on that
land. They feel also the life that might be lived on that
land and they realize that this life can be lived only in the
true House of the American—conceived as the total cultivated scene. Thus while Europe burns America builds
in a continental collaborative adventure. The astonishing
product of design, construction, and grass-roots coöperation is the reborn life of the Tennessee Valley . . . the
Great Plains . . . the Columbia . . . the Colorado . . .
the Eleven Valleys. Theorize about the American way?
I say it is in action all over this continent; I repeat, moreover, that here are the constituents of the Great Tradition.

✓ ✓ ✓

But, enough of contemporary example of the two rival
traditions which fought, and still fight, for supremacy
over each man and each culture. To comprehend them
we must see them in conflicting action, and to that drama
we turn next.

The Eternal Problem

Had you thought that a man was all of a piece?
I know the scientists say so . . . but he is not.

Everyman is a deep dichotomy . . . he is Two Men
In everyman—
   there is authoritarian . . . and democrat,
      pragmatist . . . and poet,
      exploiter . . . and sustainer-of-the-yield.
   there is a pride of Self . . . and a sense of neighbor
      —a practical opportunism . . . and an adamant
         idealism.
   there is the aggrandizing I . . . and the balancing
      We.

But to make these two men one—
   That is the eternal problem.

Because of this split in Everyman,
Every Mediterranean culture is a corresponding di-
      chotomy.
Within each one two rival traditions contend for su-
      premacy:
   —The Exploitive Tradition of the Individualist . . .
   —The Great Tradition of the Person.

The Exploitive Tradition was the motive power
   that built our technically efficient producing
      plant . . .
   —but also endangered it by withholding it from use.

The Great Tradition mirrored the Person
and organized the Good Life.
Sensitive Prophets stated it in moving words . . .
with the gesture of the body . . .
with stone or with tone,
—with the statesmanship of social engineering,
And some turned nomad shelter into organic
architecture of the total cultivated scene.

All were concerned with sustaining the yield
—that the Individual should become the Person.

But to make these two traditions one—
That . . . is the eternal problem.

Three

THE EXPLOITIVE TRADITION

The Individual and the Democratic Constellation of Ideas

He that would understand the current crisis must grasp the dynamic ideas that produced our democratic-industrial civilization in three millennia of history. I mean the common body of ideas which motivated both the Exploitive Tradition that built the civilization and the Great Tradition that idealized and sublimated it. They can be organized most clearly as a powerful cluster that generated from one nuclear concept—

The Supreme Value of the Individual

His Freedoms
His Work and Property
His Equalities
His Expression
His Communal Relationships

This is the constellation of ideas that drove western men on to build their respective ways of life, their codes of law and morals, their social systems, philosophies, and religions. And these are the key ideas in the superb pre-

51

ambles of their major state papers. From Magna Carta to the New Economic Bill of Rights one note rings out in every edition of the People's Charter: the freedoms of each human being in the multitude of individuals . . . his right to property and to work . . . his right to the equality of sovereignty of his and the others' personalities . . . his right to live his own life, making his own statement . . . his right to pursue happiness in his own unique way. These ideas all spring from the same basic concept—the Supreme Value of the Individual.

The Ancestry of the Idea

The concept that the Individual has supreme value in himself was becoming increasingly acceptable to approximately all the peoples of the world, at least until the current interregnum of Fascist governments turned the main line of advancing Democracy back toward the tangent of One-Man Totalitarianism. The ancient Mediterranean peoples and especially the Indo-Europeans appear to have played the leading role in inventing and disseminating the great idea, thereby "individualizing" the earth. Not only in twenty-five "new" countries, where the European Nordic and Latin went after 1500 A.D., but in the Oriental half of the world as well, the dignity and worth of the Individual men and women was instrumentalized by the group . . . Family . . . Clan . . . Tribe . . . Nation . . . State. Indeed, the rise of industrial-democratic civilization and the childhood and adolescence of the concept of the Individual were concurrent.

Our scholars are making a sophisticated statement of this great cluster of ideas,[1] as it has been developed for

[1] No phenomenon of our creative years is more important than that

more than 3000 years of Mediterranean-European history in two cultural currents of practical action and creative thought. The first—the EXPLOITIVE TRADITION—was the obvious stream of practical civilization-building. It produced the brilliant invention of instruments of thought— the modern languages, measuring devices, the higher mathematics and the scientific method . . . the daring exploration of seas and continents . . . the clearance and settlement of land and the building of systems of agriculture, industry, trade, government, education, social organization. This is man's unending conflict over property and government, the rise and fall of economic-social classes and of nations and nation-states. This is the

of the new interpretations that are being made by a considerable body of brilliant contemporary students of our social order. To name only a few of the clearest current examples: W. T. Stace's *The Destiny of Western Man* (Reynal and Hitchcock, 1942), James Feibleman's *Positive Democracy* (University of North Carolina Press, 1940), Waldo Frank's *Chart for Rough Water* (Doubleday Doran, 1940), Pitrim Sorokin's *The Crisis of Our Age* (E. P. Dutton, 1941). These "realist" philosophers—"profane" as well as "sacred"—all dig into the two to three thousand year-long egocentric, economic, political, social, esthetic roots of modern life. Mr. Feibleman concentrates on the economic roots, Mr. Stace on moral roots, Mr. Frank on cosmic roots, and Mr. Sorokin on a study of the cyclic movement of culture periods. Taken together, they are building the historical foundations for a modern metaphysics and social religion.

What "professed" philosophers put their minds to when the world's greatest war brings them together, is shown best, I think, in the *Symposium on Science, Philosophy and Religion*, prepared by a group of several hundred professors and students who attended the three Conferences held in New York City in 1940, 1941 and 1942. Nobel prize winners in science, Protestant and Catholic theologians, historians, anthropologists and sociologists, directors of art museums, pragmatist philosophers of the scientific method, deans of letters and classical studies voluntarily came together under the threat of totalitarianism to democracy to probe the philosophic roots of our crisis. "Pragmatists" en-masse . . . a few exponents of a fine intuitive sense in religion . . . but far too few Poets.

clash of competing political structures: government by One Man or a Few Men against the varieties of Democracy—that is, government by Many Men.

This practical, building, organizational stream of life, with its emphasis upon preëmption and competitive private ownership, was Individualism on the march—rugged as well as ragged individualism. It built the magnificent physical structure of modern civilization—the beautiful communities of Euro-American villages, towns, and cities, and the powerful producing systems. But it also brought on the earth their corresponding horrid slums and stalled factories and farms. Both ruggedly strong and beautiful and raggedly anemic and ugly stands the outcome today. I shall call it *The Exploitive Tradition,* partly to call attention to the spirit of physical construction which built a better material world than man had ever known before, but also to point to the orgy of waste, of mining the land and the people, the recurring violation of the sustained-yield principle.

The other expression of the powerful intellectual constellation was the stream of creative thought and feeling that, in company with other students of western culture, I shall call THE GREAT TRADITION.[2] In contrast to the pragmatic stream of Individualism which gripped most of the people, this creative current was restricted to a smaller nucleus of sensitive men. It was the imaginative, poetic,

[2] See especially the brilliant twenty-year long statement by Mr. Waldo Frank. Frank's most rounded systematic account of the Great Tradition in western culture is *Chart for Rough Water,* but the reader should not miss the chapter on "The Atlantic World" in *America Hispana* which is the best of his cultural portraits (in the low-priced edition called *South of Us* see especially pp. 309-350), as well as his *Rediscovery of America . . . In the American Jungle . . . Salvos.*

religious idealization of the good life that could be lived. Its ancestry can be traced to three mother cultures which grew in the eastern Mediterranean in the first millennium before Christ and the first centuries thereafter. Its documents were meagerly recorded by the first Hebrew prophets in the Old Testament—Moses, Amos, Isaiah, Hosea . . . by Jesus and Paul and the early Christians in the New Testament, all of whom, as Mr. Waldo Frank says, "made a contribution so revolutionary that it is hard to conceive. Within the communal life they stressed the responsibility of the man. The work and destiny of the nation has its fulcrum in the Individual. Justice also and service to God become individual matters."

Other pre-Christian records of this spirit and idea were recorded by the great Greeks, in sensitive esthetic expression, and in a kind of ivory-tower intellectual design of democratic government. Socrates, Plato and Aristotle, and their artist compatriots—Phidias, and the builders, Aeschylus, Sophocles, and Euripides and the men of the theatre arts—are luminous examples. They gave us brilliant intellectual analyses of the root idea of the Individual, but in practice their political democracy was restricted to the free citizens in a slave-society, and of social democracy they had practically nothing.

Religious thinkers in the early Christian centuries tried to put the concept of the dignity and worth of the individual into social practice. Historical scholarship applied to such records as the Talmud and the New Testament [3]

---

[3] See, for example, in *The Symposium on Science, Philosophy and Religion* (1941 conference) the work of such students as Albert C. Outler: "The Patristic Christian Ethos and Democracy" (Chapter XXVI), Millar Burrows: "Democracy in the Hebrew-Christian Tradition; Old and New Testaments" (Chapter XXIII) and Ben Zion

shows that although political democracy as a particular form of government does not appear, what does appear is the deep seated conviction of the worth and rights of every man from the king to the meanest peasant. As Professor Burrows says: "It is from the Hebrew-Christian tradition that we receive the conception of the intrinsic value of every human individual which makes the idea of democracy real and worthy of our devotion."

Slowly, very slowly, the conception took hold of the more sensitive men, but only rarely among the more rugged and aggrandizing ones who came to be the leaders of the Nordic tribes that settled around and within the Roman empire before 1500 A.D. and built the first nations and nation-states. Then through 1500 years of Europe-building the great western rivals of mood and philosophy—the Exploitive Tradition and the Great Tradition—fought for each man's mind and soul and for domination over each group culture. Measured by the numbers that were conquered, the Exploitive Tradition —with its lure of comfort and power and glory—won out. Most men were captured by the practical tasks of farming, building, producing, merchandising, governing, healing, in short, by the rewards of the economic and social institutions of the people.

THE EXPLOITIVE TRADITION

The documentation of the new historians makes very clear that the industrial-democratic society built in some seven or eight hundred years by a dynamic body of western Europeans was primarily an individualistic so-

Bokser: "Democratic Aspirations in Talmudic Judaism" Chapter XXII.)

cial order based on competitive business. In scene after scene the peoples of the world have struggled to get an ever better living from the earth. In the center of every episode have been two or more competing individualists, each driven by the desire for a better living, each wanting security, personal power and social prestige, each one feeling and many of them saying: "That's mine, I saw it first, I put my mark on it. You can't take it, you can't encroach on it, indeed, you tax it at your peril." Rugged individualism . . . the chronic presence of egocentrism in humanity—that is the spirit of the Exploitive Tradition.

The result was, as the very appellations given to our civilization by its critical students indicate, a business civilization: an acquisitive society . . . a pecuniary civilization . . . a competitive social order.[4] It was the achievement of the urban business men of north Italy, Germany, France, Flanders, Holland, Britain, after the twelfth century A.D. and of the twenty-five "new" countries which they founded around the globe after 1600 A.D. The leadership in the building of the new industrial society and its political government was assumed by a modern business fraternity of manufacturers, financiers, and middle men and their inventors and managers. In each of the growing trading towns—from north Italy in the twelfth and thirteenth centuries through south Germany in the fourteenth to sixteenth, then along the

[4] A vast and growing library of original documents is well epitomized in such secondary sources as the output of a generation of "new historians": e.g. Professors Tawney, Laski, Cole, Hobsons and others of the London School of Economics and Political Science; such Americans as Veblen, Turner, Robinson, the three Beards, Thomas, Barnes, Dewey, Whitehead, Mead, Feibleman, Sorokin.

west coast of Europe, in the British Isles and in the Americas, Australias, New Zealand, and South Africa. History repeated itself in all these centers; the business fraternity —or middle class, technically known as the bourgeoisie— secured economic power and governed as well, even if behind the political scene. Gradually the idea of government by Divine-Right-Hereditary-Kings was supplanted by the idea of government by a small group of property owners—first, by the owners of Big Property, and later extended to a larger group of owners of Small Property. But by 1800 "Divine Right" was pretty well out of the saddle.

During the nineteenth and twentieth centuries, in different places around the earth and in varying degrees, political control was extended to a considerably larger proportion of the population. Slowly in centers like middle Europe and Latin America, more rapidly in others like the British Commonwealth of Nations, and most rapidly of all, we Americans feel, in our own country the foundations of democratic government were laid and great charters expressive of the Individual were written into history.

The Exploitive Tradition, The Freedoms, and Property

Because industrialism was primarily a competitive individualistic social order two of our cluster of democratic ideas played the central role in the building of the Exploitive Tradition: the special definition of the idea of freedom of the Individual as absence of restraint, and the idea of his right to the ownership and preëmption of property. In an acquisitive society, property—its possession, enhancement, and inheritance—is the primary interest in the lives of its leaders, and the protection of its private ownership becomes their central endeavor. The land owners of the countryside and especially in recent years the financial, manufacturing, trading owners of the towns took care to guarantee the legal protection of their ownership by taking over the control of government. The property owners justified this seizure of control by establishing their "rights" in great state charters.

But by no means were all the freedoms asked for or secured at any single cataclysmic moment. A glance back over their history shows the slow process by which the freedoms evolved—first in one aspect of the individual's life and then in another. There are three distinct types:

1. the civil freedoms—those that deal with individuals as persons,
2. the political freedoms—those that deal with the individual's participation in collective affairs,
3. the economic freedoms—those that deal with the individual's relations to property and work.

But only for the first two of these was there successful agitation until our own day.

With the appearance of vast economic changes about the beginning of the twelfth century came the idea that the individual should be left free to work out his own salvation in every ramification of his life. By the thirteenth century the trend had reached such proportions that a small determined group of English land owners could compel John of England to sign Magna Carta. That charter, as we know, abounds in the word "free." From that time to today the literature of great political documents is filled with stipulations of freedom. To call to our minds only a few of the conspicuous ones: the British Petition of Right (1628) and Bill of Rights (1688) . . . the American Declaration of Independence (1776) . . . the French Declaration of the Rights of Man (1791) . . . the Chinese Sun Yat-Sen's Three Principles of the People (1911) . . . The Mexican Constitution (1917) . . . The Constitution of the U.S.S.R. (1918) . . . and the Constitution of the German Republic (1919).

Since throughout all history ambitious and shrewd men created economic freedom for themselves we would expect the concept of property, its ownership and control, to play an important part in the life history of the "freedoms." But the codification of the idea was not achieved in the charters of liberty until our own day. In the current proposals of our leaders to establish new freedoms we can see the contemporary stage in the history of this spirit of individualism that provided the motive power for the new western society. Mr. Roosevelt's Four Freedoms and Mr. Wallace's interpretation of them . . . the National Resources Planning Board's New Economic Bill of Rights—the "Nine Freedoms" . . . and the Atlantic Charter—are examples of our attempt to make sure that this time social convulsion shall guarantee freedom in *every* walk of life.

"Freedom" as Defined by the Exploitive Tradition: Absence of Restraint

It is of the utmost importance that we note the contrast in the definition of freedom by the Exploitive Tradition and by the Great Tradition, and that I shall document in this chapter and the following one. During the First Industrial Revolution, our European property-owning fathers, seeking freedom from their hereditary rulers and the "mercantile" regulations to do as they pleased with things or men, had just one definition in mind. That was —absence of restraint. From Magna Carta to the Reform Bills of the nineteenth century the successive charters of liberty consist essentially in removing restraints of individual action in widening areas of life. This, as students of western society agree, went far toward producing the conquering, building stream of western life which I have called the Exploitive Tradition. But in its train came widespread social evils and corresponding vigorous efforts to remedy them. In the past two generations these have led to the building of a less individualistic and more socialized spirit, a modern version of the Great Tradition, the intellectual center of which is a new definition of freedom. To note this shift in orientation let us document briefly the development of the idea of freedom in the First Industrial Revolution.

1. THE PERSONAL AND PSYCHOLOGICAL (CIVIL) FREEDOMS

—*Freedom of movement . . . restraint taken off* the individual's right to come and go . . . in some hundreds of years serfdom slowly disappeared . . . body slavery was ended in Russia (white) and in America (black) as late as the 1860s. This made possible the mobility needed for industrial civilization. It was mere "lip service" to true freedom of movement, however, for to the present day the purchasing power needed to come and go has not been guaranteed. Not until complete economic freedom is established will freedom of movement be a reality.

—*Freedom of public assembly*—*restraints removed* from free men wanting to take thought together for personal growth and participation in collective life. Psychological restraints are still imposed today, however, in all cases in which lack of economic security creates fears and inhibits appearance in public assemblies.

—*Freedom of speech* . . . *restraint removed* from the individual's right to speak, write, or otherwise publish his own ideas. Few practice it, however, because the majority lack real economic freedom and are held back by fear of consequences.

—*Freedom of worship* . . . *restraints removed* from the right to worship as one wishes. But psychological inhibitions are still evident in certain intimate face-to-face communities.

—*Freedom of habeas corpus and trial by a jury of one's peers* . . . *removing restraints* of unjust arrest, imprisonment, trial and punishment . . . goes far toward releasing the individual from psychological restraints on his actions. But because of the lag of understanding in the general population the effectiveness of this system still leaves much to be desired.

These brief examples illustrate that in seven hundred years of advancing civil liberties the chief concern of the aggressive individuals who demanded and secured them was about the removal of personal restraints. Thus freedom was defined as absence of restraint.

2. FREEDOMS OF GOVERNMENT—POLITICAL AND PSYCHOLOGICAL

The story of advancing political rights parallels that of personal freedom. In the early centuries of industrial-democratic history selected persons, favored by accidents of birth in homes of wealth, intelligence, or political strength, were given special advantages of political participation. Their freedoms were to take part in public discussion and policy-making . . . to vote for one's preferred representatives in government . . . to criticize policies and policy-making and legislative, executive, and judicial acts . . . to initiate discussion and action leading to the continuous amendment and reconstruction of constitutions, laws, and regulations . . . to hold office in government if chosen by one's fellows.

Slowly at first, but rapidly after 1800 A.D., the major political liberties were extended to an increasing proportion of the people, irrespective of property ownership and economic-social affiliations. As that took place freedom was still defined as absence of restraint: freedom from restraint on the initiation of discussion and action leading to the making of constitutions, laws, regulations . . . freedom from restraint on the criticism of government policies and policy-making . . . freedom from the personal restraint of employers over employees . . . of fathers over children . . . of powerful citizens or groups over weaker ones in the community.

It is important to bear in mind this definition of freedom that was characteristic of the first half dozen centuries of advancing democratic life, not only because of the marked change that is coming about in our own time, but also because today ultra-free enterprisers and the normalcy-isolationist press demand its re-instatement as the only solution of our economic problems. And that brings us to the economic freedoms.

3. THE ECONOMIC FREEDOMS

LAISSEZ-FAIRE——FREEDOM TO EXPLOIT PROPERTY
AND, BY IMPLICATION, THE PEOPLE

As I said a while back, under the influence of the Exploitive Tradition, the economic freedoms were not
written into constitutions. But they came to be discussed
in theoretical books on economics and political science
in the latter part of the eighteenth century, when the
physiocrats of Louis XV's court phrased the philosophy
of *laissez-faire* and Adam Smith, professor of moral philosophy at the University of Glasgow, gave world-wide
circulation to the idea by publishing his book *Inquiry
into the Nature and Causes of the Wealth of Nations.*
This new "Declaration of Independence for Industry,"
published in 1776, advised governments to leave each individual free to compete with every other one and to
use his initiative and intelligence in preëmpting and exploiting all the natural resources. Let the economic system develop free from government and it will produce
the greatest wealth for the nation; total wealth was
meant—the theory did not plan for redistribution of the
wealth among the people.

This one idea—*laissez-faire*—gripped the business men
of the western world through many centuries. For a
thousand years they told kings and premiers, presidents
and congresses: "Let us alone!" It is now a truism of history that this guiding slogan of action, even if unphrased,
motivated the millions of pioneers who cleared North and
South America, Australia, New Zealand, South Africa,
and the islands of the entire earth between 1780 and

1880. Under the drive of this idea the coal, iron and other minerals, the forests, the soil, the vegetation all were taken in an orgy of exploitation. Public utilities were created that bound a hundred thousand communities together. This economic concept—each individual for himself—domineered over the entire First Industrial Revolution.

Property Was Defined Negatively

Through hundreds of years of history as the Great Society was put together by the entrepreneurs and their lawyers, scientists and inventors, ecclesiasts and theocrats, the democratic outlook took form. The nub was the modern concept of property, defined through countless legal contests, parliamentary debates, executive fiats and other specific acts of overt behavior. This centering of man's behavior on property was to be expected, no doubt, in a culture in which *things* were so domineeringly in the saddle. Witness the principal steps of the argument: It was a business, pecuniary, competitive civilization, created by the new middle-class entrepreneurs, the bourgeoisie, whose major interest was the acquisition of property and the accumulation of things, and the security, power and prestige that were their accompaniment. The concept of *laissez-faire* led the individual to say "I got here first. I preëmpted it. It's mine. I invented it . . . organized it, created it, it's mine." To the people caught in such a climate of opinion the "real" things of life were houses, ships, factories, money, offices in government, and their paper signs—stocks and bonds, treasury certificates, checks, and notes.

As Professor Sorokin has reminded us in his brilliant

four volumes,[5] on the time-line of history our modern industrial society constitutes one of the great recurring cycles of "sensate" culture. It is a culture in which things are valued most highly, in which science and philosophy tend to become utilitarian, psychology a physiology of the nervous system, and religion a social gospel. To know in order to control becomes the supreme end of behavior and education becomes little more than trade schools devoted to the useful arts and crafts. In such a sensate culture property, like other democratic ideas, tends to be defined negatively, in terms of things, physical particulars, instead of positively in terms of their use.[6]

The history of law in western society is replete with the evidence of property defined as substance—as the thing; modern law indeed was founded upon the law of property. But that was necessarily a negative definition. The right to own meant the restrictive right to preëmpt, to keep others off. (I rode a thousand miles in a motor car on the veldt of the Union of South Africa . . . another thousand around the rim of Australia, rarely seeing a house, a cultivated ranch—and rarely leaving a wire fence! Land preëmpted, but not used.) Witness the millions of "no trespassing" placards . . . the patent law— "I invented that, no one can use it without my permission" . . . the copyright law—"No reproduction of more than thirty words without the permission of the

[5] Pitirim Sorokin: *Social and Cultural Dynamics* (American Book Company, 1936-1941); see also the single interpretative volume of the documentary studies: *The Crisis of Our Age* (Dutton, 1941).

[6] For the clearest statement of this negative nominalistic interpretation we are indebted to the work of one of the most independent and alert free-lance philosophic minds of our day—to Mr. James Feibleman's *Positive Democracy* (University of North Carolina Press, 1941).

publisher" . . . the law of priority of discovery—"I found that (or at least my grandfather did) . . . it's mine."

We need not multiply illustrations. Is it not clear that throughout the First Industrial Revolution property—one of the great cornerstones of our culture—was defined as substance, as thing. It was defined negatively, protecting the owner's right to withhold it from use.

Equality, Communal Relationships, and Expression of the Individual[7] in the Exploitive Tradition

The third great concept in the democratic constellation is equality, an idea that occupies a central place in the preambles to the great charters of liberty in modern times. However, most of these state papers were written in a society captured by the Exploitive Tradition. That tradition did not implement the "equality" concept by guaranteeing a national minimum of purchasing power —and there was no other way to implement it. Hence while giving lip service to the concept of Equality the politicians who administered the governments, failed miserably, and still fail in fact, to practice it. Equality under the Exploitive Tradition does not mean "we are all Supremes." It means, "I am superior . . . You are Inferior, and I shall rule you."

Only in 1942, for example, in the midst of a war for our democratic existence, did we change our practice of refusing to let Chinese seamen, our allies, debark in our

[7] Because of the narrow interpretation given to the three remaining ideas of the democratic constellation by the Exploitive Tradition, their discussion here is brief, for their fuller positive analysis, turn to Chapter IV.

ports and mingle with the "white" men and women on our city streets. Today we disenfranchise millions of citizens born with colored skins and their white brothers in poverty. We refuse to let Negroes register in our hotels . . . we compel them to move from our suburban communities . . . we refuse them access to our new housing projects. We discriminate against persons of specified church affiliations. Our newspapers are full of advertising of "restricted" summer hotels. We bar non-whites from learned "honor" societies. And our British allies still exercise imperialistic rule over 380,000,000 East Indians, and insist that The Atlantic Charter's proclamation of a free world does not mean them.

Do we practice the concept that "all men are created equal?" We do not. This is the Exploitive Tradition in action. This is man's inhumanity to man and To-day's war abroad as well as Tomorrow's war at home is being fought over this issue as well as over the obvious ones of the international and economic freedoms. It is high time that our people realize that we shall lose our allies in the Asian continent unless we rid ourselves of our antipathies and our fears born of our false superiorities, and make up our minds to implement the word "all" in the Declaration. Every step which we take in that direction will move us away from the Exploitive Tradition.

↗ ↗ ↗

As for the concept of the necessary communal relationships of the individual: one of the most important factors that will instate the Great Tradition in modern times is the growing socialization of the spirit of the people. I shall not anticipate here my fuller positive discussion of the factors of the social process. But we should at least remind ourselves at this point that this spirit is being born of the recurring breakdowns of the economic system and the sensing by more and more people of the tenuous character of industrial society and of the need for social controls.

It was characteristic of the aggrandizing buccaneers who played fast and loose in the First Industrial Revolution that they were utterly insensitive to the interdependence of modern men. Above all else they affirmed their self-sufficiency, their independence, their resourcefulness. They proclaimed Manifest Destiny. They dared nature to deny their mastery. They minimized the integrity of the individual, barely recognized the necessity of social communion, had little feeling for expressive life. Neighbor raced against neighbor for the rewards of work. As a consequence they produced at the turn of the twentieth century a western culture of widespread hypocrisy, and downright exploitation of men as well as things. This too was the Exploitive Tradition in action.

✓ ✓ ✓

The final idea in the cluster that defines the Supreme Value of the Individual is the guarantee of his right, freedom, and stimulation to express himself . . . to live and let live . . . to make his own statement of life as he sees it, feels it, and wants to live it. Not only is each man an individualist in the sense of wanting to be relieved of restraint, but as our everyday lives prove, each man also feels deeply the drive to get himself stated: the hand craftsman works and saves to set up his little shop, the young librarian her own little bookstore, the housewife her home. The painter, the poet, the novelist, the dramatist, the creative artist generally—each is trying to express life as he sees it. Whether naive or sophisticated, every human being has the urge to put into some objective form what he is and feels at a given moment. This is indeed the mark of our expressive age.

Did the Exploitive Tradition of the First Industrial Revolution create conditions favorable to this expressive process? It did not. On the contrary, it created an emotional climate of competition, of insecurity, of fear of neighbor, of hurried and shoddy work, of quantity rather than quality, of respect for the classic standards and styles of other cultures and other times, of building well-enough-to-get-by rather than doing one's best job, of hypocrisy rather than integrity. Again, this was the Exploitive Tradition in action. A Reminder!

If at this point my reader protests: "But this is a negative, lopsided interpretation of the roots of our American Way!" I reply: This is *one* of the two deep-running strands of the American Way—the Exploitive Tradition. This is the side that is basically negative, although superficially positive. This is the aggrandizing, conquering, materialistic side that captured men on both sides of the Atlantic during the First Industrial Revolution.

Do not forget the admonition with which we began this study:

Everyman is a deep dichotomy . . . he is Two Men . . .

Exploiter and Sustainer-of-the Yield . . . aggrandizing **I** . . . and balancing **We**.

And do not forget—that—

Every Mediterranean culture is a corresponding dichotomy. Within each one two rival traditions contend for supremacy
—The Exploitive Tradition of the Individualist . . .
—The Great Tradition of the Person.

But my reader's protests are actually buttressed by the pageant of history. This Exploitive Tradition in the American Way *was* the motive power that built our technically efficient producing plant:

—Egocentric, aggressive individualists impelled by the lure of a better living, personal power, and social prestige . . .
—having secured their civil and political freedoms, took their economic freedom in hand . . .
—and made the greatest attack in the history of mankind of the miner on the rich and virgin land . . . preëmpted well-nigh the entire globe, cleared it and built on it the producing structure of an industrial civilization that for the first time in all Man's history could give him physical abundance.

Magnificent Positive Achievements

My conviction that now is the moment to take the key step in turning a potentially abundant civilization into an actual one is born in part of the thrill I get in appraising the brilliant achievement of our fathers of the First Industrial Revolution. It is difficult indeed to restrain one's language and not to turn appreciative appraisal into fulsome eulogy. For it was a magnificent positive achievement, even in meagerest outline review the record is astounding:

Out of their prolonged creative ordeal covering centuries of effort the men of science in the Great Tradition[8]

---

[8] The reader may wish to scan, at this point, the more extensive documentation of the contribution of the Euro-Americans of the

Great Tradition in Chapter IV.

passed on to us five instruments of precise thought by which at this—our moment—it is possible to produce a degree of order in our disorganized world:

—modern languages of great complexity and subtle power of meaning,
—concepts and instruments of more precise measurement,
—mathematical methods of detecting and stating relationships,
—the concept and process of scientific method and of inquiry and work,
—institutions of creative research and dissemination of ideas.

The practical inventors, technicians, managers, organizers, and marketers used these instruments to replace wooden machines turned by wind and water wheels with mile-square, straight-line, automatic, power-machine factories. One can have nothing but admiration for a creative mind that can turn a creaking inefficient age of wood-and-leather into one of steel, aluminum-magnesium alloys and plastics and near-manless production of quantity goods. A mind imaginative enough to conceive these three foundations of efficient machine-technology:

1. Engines—"prime movers"—that produce and transmit power mechanically, with 90-odd per cent efficiency.
2. Machines of manipulative cleverness.
3. Vertical corporations concentrating financial support and integrating all necessary processes of manufacture in a single "straight-line" factory system.

A mind that can invent such necessary contributory processes as these: new, tough, flexible materials . . . new fuels and plants necessary to treat the materials . . .

powerful, precise machine tools and measuring instruments . . . an army of technicians and skilled workers . . . a central factory integrating all related manufacturing processes . . . a climate of opinion of workers working for wages . . . and a world-wide marketing system. Most of this has happened in less than two centuries, and the most spectacular gains of all have come since the close of the First Industrial Revolution, approximately fifty years ago.

My conviction that the democratic peoples can create an organized free world out of the anarchy of today is born of the knowledge and appreciation of this brilliant foundational achievement. In spite of the current inhumanity and chaos, the new Individualism produced the world's highest standard of living. It more than doubled the length of life . . . cut western man's hours of labor in half . . . markedly reduced pain and fatigue . . . provided an exciting variety of things to do in the new leisure of the common man . . . advanced his enlightenment and started him questioning his superstitions . . . partially dismissed the ownership of slave bodies and initiated the ousting of economic slavery . . . increased the radius of social sympathy through world-wide means of communication.

As a consequence the material result today of all-out employment and production under war conditions is breath-taking: a million tons of ships a month . . . a four-engine bomber every hour . . . a hundred thousand airplanes a year . . . $125,000,000,000 annual national income . . . an air-minded, world-minded, efficient, production-conscious American people learning not to be afraid of running their economic system without regard to traditional concepts of the "bookkeeping costs."

As Hitler began to wreak his evil on civilization at the end of the first third of the twentieth century,

> Creative Americans were drawing the curtain aside
> On a vista of world communal life
> . . . of a civilization just over the horizon
> whose wealth, beauty and spirit
> Will stagger the imagination and dwarf anything that
> has gone before.

But the fact that the man called Hitler, could wreak his evil is a full measure of the inadequacy of the Exploitive Tradition to build the Good Life. For not only was it true that

> The Exploitive Tradition was the motive power
> that built our technically efficient producing plant,
> *but*, it also—
> *endangered it by withholding it from use.*

Indeed, in the twentieth century the Exploitive Tradition brought the world to the destruction of many of the great social gains and to the threshold of a dark, miserable impasse. Not until a compact minority of the American people grasp the meaning of what the Exploitive Tradition really did, and act upon that knowledge will the Great Tradition and the now-possible Good Life come alive on this continent. And this is the moment for all who understand it to teach it and do something about it with despatch.

THE ETERNAL PROBLEM

The impasse we confront today is really two-fold. There is nearer the surface of our lives the immediate problem of the practical adjustment of an aggrandizing I and a balancing We. This is the nub of our Two Wars —Today's War Abroad . . . Tomorrow's War at home. Although staggeringly complex, it is simple compared to the other and more subtle one to be solved in our day. That other one, setting the longer-time task and the chief educational problem for our children, is the discovery of how—

> To make these two men—the exploiter
> and the sustainer of the yield—
> to make these two men one.

And to make these two traditions one.

That . . . is the eternal problem.

It is the problem of sublimating egocentrism into the idealism of human nature—thus producing ideal democracy on a high philosophical and religious level.

Since I shall deal with the more profound problem in subsequent chapters, I confine my comments here to the more immediate practical problem. This is the one we shall face at the successive moments of the armistices in Today's war abroad: namely to find out how much more social capital and social control shall be interjected into our American individualistic life.

THE CRUX: "I" AND "WE"

We should think of this problem that has baffled men throughout civilized history in terms of its proper dictionary name——THE CRUX. I am convinced that it is the most crucial practical human issue—the problem of how two or more aggrandizing I's can work out a balancing We. It is the age-long problem of Freedom and Control . . . of the Individual and the Culture . . . of Self and Society . . . of Private and Public. Although its psychological effects ramify through every aspect of family, neighborhood, community, and national life, the nature of the impasse today is essentially economic.

The question we must answer is simply this:

How much social control do we have to impose upon individuals to operate our economic system and yet preserve the American idea of—
"Let me be the one to do what is done."

. . .

"Keep off each other and keep each other off." [9]

More baldly put:
How much government and how much private enterprise and in between, how much "coöperatives"?

The Incompetence of Man, Working Alone

When you bring all the factors of the Exploitive Tradition together and strip them down to barest essentials, this, it seems to me, is what has happened—most of it since 1600 A.D.:

Millions of intelligent courageous seekers-after-the-better-land-over-yonder . . . were turned loose on the richest virgin continents of the globe. This was under a principle of social action that gave them complete free-

[9] As Robert Frost so beautifully put it in two separate lines in "Build Soil."

dom to preëmpt the dazzling natural riches . . . and under a definition of freedom and of property that permitted them to develop, to build, to waste, or to sustain-the-yield, to take immediate or deferred profits, or to withhold the land entirely from the use of other men.

But the process of man's putting those principles into action has laid bare two new sets of data about the incompetence of man as a lone worker—his violation of the sustained-yield principle and the vast spread of individual differences among men. I bring them up not only because they lie at the very roots of the current impasse, but also because they have not received sufficient attention by those who aspire to lead in the education of our people. The first of these two sets of data deals with the human individualist's notorious inability to restrain his desire for immediate profits . . . his unwillingness to spread the fat years' surplus over the lean years' deficit . . . his incapacity to sustain the yield either of land or men.

There is something in a man that distrusts the deferred security of Tomorrow . . . "a bird in the hand *is* worth two in the bush" . . . "anyway, nature is boundless" . . . "there's better land over yonder" . . . "I need not take thought for tomorrow." The impulse is to take now, ignoring the fact that your competing neighbor is of the same human flesh and blood.

The record of history bears out the homely truisms of practical philosophers. In the building of every major national civilization—the British, the German, the French, the Japanese, the American—strong individualists exploited quickly both the land and the people. In a two century long orgy of construction they settled on the sub-humid land, over-cut and over-burned the trees . . . over-plowed and over-planted the soil . . . over-grazed and over-browsed the grasses. The floods-you-don't-see gnawed away the topsoil and the floods-you-see pushed it down the rivers into the oceans. When the rains ceased the winds blew the topsoil off the continent.

Thus the Exploitive Tradition in the man and in the culture mined and eroded the land. The people too were mined—their security in the land and their job, their craftsmanship as well as purchasing power. Their security in neighborliness, in human integrity. Under the rule of *laissez-faire,* the shrewd and ambitious and vigorous Indo-Europeans came into the ownership of the things that men must have—strategic land, fuels, metals, fibers, foods, credit and transport and communication channels. In their haste for immediate profits the aggrandizing I's among the people once more forgot *the Sustained-Yield Principle:*

> *Whether it is land or people or minds you*
> *are growing—provide for a sustained yield.*
> *Build soil!*

This is the lesson of history. Wherever the sustained-yield principle was violated, the civilizations declined. Some died. So it was with China . . . with Mesopotamia . . . with India . . . with Amerindia.

Will ours decline? . . . Perhaps die? . . . We are now deciding.

In two ways I said, the newest violation of the sustained-yield principle reveals a lone man's incompetence to cope with Nature, the first being his need for "the bal-

ancing We." The second is the recurring revelation of
his incapacity to cope with his fellow men—if turned
free to race with them. The foundation of the argument
is the psychologists' famous "law of individual differences," now documented for every human trait. To
remind yourself of its validity, consider any random
human population you know: the next thousand men
who pass you on a crowded street corner . . . a movie
audience . . . the adults of a town . . . the children of
a school. Every one of these populations will reveal the
tall and the short, the strong and the weak, the brilliant
and the stupid, the domineering and the submissive, the
adventurous and the timid, the dynamic and the inert,
the imaginative and the dull; and the preponderance of
the people will lie in a great mediocrity between the two
extremes.

Now this fact of the differences in human nature, cou-
pled with geographic conditions of the land and the concepts of the Exploitive Tradition, brought about the
social crisis of modern times. History has proved once
again that human beings cannot be turned loose on the
principle of every man for himself. The American episode confirms the modern European and more ancient
Mediterranean and Oriental ones. If a number of people
start on an equal basis in any enterprise and are left free
to compete—for honors, jobs, land, money, power, prestige, what not—within a short time the few who are
shrewder, more vigorous, more ambitious and more intelligent, will come out on top with the best jobs, the
best land, most of the money and control over their fellows—in short, more of the world's goods and most of
the power and the glory. Throughout the history of civ-

ilization—the case of every tribe, clan, family, and nation of which there is any record—this has been true. So we speak of a second "law" in social psychology to accompany the "law" of individual differences.

But the fact of the "law," while interesting, is not as important as the effects it brings in its train. The strong do exploit the weak, preëmpting the land and withholding it from use. They do exemplify the negative and substance definition of freedom and property. And unless society—the "multitude of individuals"—is vigilant and sets up controls on the individual the whole system is likely to be disrupted and millions of people exploited. At least this is what has happened time after time in history. The fundamental problem arises, then, of how to operate an interdependent society of free individuals on the basis of sustaining the yield for a large number. This involves the extent to which the individual submits to control.

❧ ❧ ❧

There's something in a man, I say,
    distrusts the deferred security of tomorrow . . .
And the Exploitive Tradition runs its course.

Who Rules Whom in a World Like Ours?

Suppose someone comes near me who in rate
Of speech and thinking is so much my better
I am imposed on, silenced and discouraged.
Do I submit to being supplied by him
As the more economical producer,
More wonderful, more beautiful producer?
No, I unostentatiously move off
Far enough for my thought-flow to resume.
Thought product and food product are to me
Nothing compared to the producing of them.

Robert Frost, "BUILD SOIL" *

* From the Frost collection, *A Further Range*, p. 94. Reprinted with permission of the publisher, Henry Holt and Co.

Four

THE GREAT TRADITION

Who rules whom in a world like ours?

Do I submit to being ruled by you as the more wonderful, more economical producer? There are two answers, and they are given by the two rival traditions of western history.

The Exploitive Tradition—crystallized in its most extreme form in the Nazi creed, which takes its cue from the philosophers of the superman, Schopenhauer and Nietzsche—arranges its concepts in this sequence: Human societies are made up of individuals who vary widely . . . Most of the individuals are weak and must be ruled . . . A few, the Master Class, are strong, and wise . . . These shall rule the others, the weak . . . They create the State as the instrument of that rule, hence all the individuals become the servants of that State.

There is another answer to the question—that given by the Great Tradition: Human societies are made up of individuals who vary widely in all physical, mental and spiritual traits . . . But there is one equality among them—the dignity and worth of each . . . Hence society consists of equal sovereign personalities—each insisting on his own integrity but deeply admiring the authentic inner truth in every other one . . . All together create the State as their coöperative instrument for rule.

Juxtaposed the two philosophies say:

The Exploitive Tradition: You and I are different. I am Superior . . . You are Inferior . . . So, I shall rule you.

The Great Tradition: You and I are different . . . Yet we must live together. I am Supreme . . . You are Supreme also . . . And we shall rule together.

Who rules whom, then, in a world like ours? This is the question that is being fought out on the battle fields of the two wars . . . Today's war abroad and Tomorrow's war at home. The believers in the Great Tradition are rising all over the world to beat down the Supermen —to destroy utterly the concept of the Master Class.

Nothing is of greater importance therefore than that our people shall understand deeply the meaning of the Great Tradition.

✓ ✓ ✓

Today's social tangle of the Two Wars points to the imperative need that fundamental social and religious principles, the philosophic foundation of our social order, must be established if our people are to make their coming social decision successfully. We know now, with Mr. Waldo Frank, who has made the most profound generalizations about the Great Tradition that "we can have no adequate politics, no adequate esthetics, no adequate ethics, without an adequate metaphysic and religion." There is no doubt that make-shift decisions can be made when hostilities cease in Europe and Asia that will temporize the present situation for a part of another generation. But unless a real understanding of the roots of this problem is grasped by our leaders, a program of action built upon it, and enough of our people persuaded to go along with the leaders in carrying it out—we shall fail to win Tomorrow's war at home. If that should happen, our remaining years will be marked by recurring and worse wars and a stunted rather than an abundant life for our people.

In each century of western history our fathers restated for their cultures and their times the Supreme Value of the Individual. To see what this Great Tradition of western man can give us at this moment we return to our study of the basic cluster of democratic ideas. For these lie at the center of the Great Tradition of the human individual and his relation to other individuals, even as they did in the Exploitive Tradition.

The Supreme Value of the Individual

His freedoms
His property and his work
His equalities
His communal relationships
His expression

I. The Freedoms Redefined

Throughout most of the First Industrial Revolution the Exploitive Tradition's definition of freedom, namely, "absence of restraint," worked not too badly; it secured not only the statement of our civil and political freedoms in the charters of liberty, but also their practice in the actual administration of social affairs. However, economic freedom was never stated until the sharp social changes in the closing years of the First Industrial Revolution compelled new laws, new practices and hence new concepts with which to think through the problems of new times.

Governing power had increasingly gone with economic power. Industrial society became a money economy and a complex of corporate enterprises with wide dissemination of small units of ownership. All this resulted in a drastic shift in the source of and route to control—the increasing separation of control from ownership—and a corresponding shift in the prizes over which men fought in the economic and political arenas.

The recent history of I and We, therefore, is the story of how the American people have actually redefined freedom of enterprise. It was not done by conscious preachment or theorizing, nor by constitutional amendment. The record is rather one of the year-by-year accretion of political events—new laws . . . new judicial decisions and administrative edicts . . . the creation of new types of controlling governmental boards, commissions, bureaus . . . the interjection of social capital into the economic system through "government yardstick corporations." Looking back upon it, we recognize a four-fold advance in control over free enterprise:

—the primary regulation of business enterprise through anti-trust laws, fixing of minimum wages and maximum hours, factory conditions, tariffs, prices, income taxes, the control of profits, the regulation of child labor, standardizing the quality of foods, drugs, and the like
—government control of private business—but without ownership of the property—through the regulation of new investment
—outright government ownership itself, as in the creation of "government yardstick corporations"—on the order of

the TVA and the other national land and water reclamation reconstructional "Authorities"
—government ownership of the tools of production, administration by private enterprise

So far has this actual redefinition of the economic freedoms already proceeded that today at least a third of our
group life is socially managed. The American people,
adamant in defense of freedom the American Way, not
only do not object that this encroaches on their freedoms, but, on the contrary, believe that in our interdependent world it actually gives them greater freedom.
Witness the necessity—because of the proved dangers to
the public good of trying to manage such affairs pri-
vately—of actual "socialization" in such aspects of modern industrialized life as water supplies, fire and health
protection, highways and bridges, schools, museums,
parks, and the regional and national control of harbors,
rivers and docks, the effects of flood and drouth. Schools
have for more than a generation been ninety-odd percent
publicly owned and operated and more than half of our
municipal power plants are today publicly owned. One
could plot on the time-line of the curve of political invention scores of laws and administrative acts that document this redefinition of free enterprise.[1]

[1] For example, in the impositions of new forms of taxes like the
Federal Income Tax (1913) and in the establishment of new regula-
tory agencies: Federal Reserve Board and Federal Trade Commission
(1914) . . . Federal Shipping Board, Federal Farm Bureau, and the
United States Tariff Commission (1916) . . . Inland Waterways Corporation and the United States Employment Service (1917) . . . Federal Power Commission (1920) . . . Grain Futures Administration
(1922) . . . Personnel Classification Board (1923) . . . Federal Radio
Commission (1927) . . . Federal Farm Board (1928). I give only a
few of the conspicuous examples of the many government controls

Moreover, as the social system of the industrialized world increased in interdependence and stalled in more frequent and deeper depressions, students and publicists demanded that economic freedom—particularly the right to work—should receive guarantees in the great charters of liberty as had been done in the case of the civil and political freedoms. And now in our great transitional period the indispensable role of the economic-social freedoms is definitely being recognized in national constitutions.[2]

Perhaps the most conspicuous statement of the freedoms necessary to the good life—the social and esthetic as well as the economic ones—is our National Resources Planning Board's New Bill of Rights, or "Nine Freedoms":

1. The right to work, usefully and creatively through the productive years.
2. The right to fair pay, adequate to command the necessities and amenities of life in exchange for work, ideas, thrift, and other socially valuable service.
3. The right to adequate food, clothing, shelter, and medical care.

that were imposed before the New Deal came to power in 1933. Because examples of controls over the economic life of the nation became so voluminous after 1933 I cannot take the space even to remind my readers of the details.

[2] In the Mexican constitution (1917): "No one may be prevented from practicing any honest profession, or from engaging in any legitimate industry, business or labor" (Article 4). In the constitution of the pre-Nazi German Republic (1919): "Every German is to be given the possibility to earn his living by economic work," when such an opportunity is not available, "his necessary maintenance will be provided for," (Article 163) and further, owners are obligated to use their property for the public good (Article 153). In the Russian constitution (1936): "Citizens in the USSR have the right to work, that is, the right to guaranteed employment and payment for their work in accordance with its quantity and quality (Article 118).

4. The right to security, with freedom from fear of old age, want, dependency, sickness, unemployment, and accident.

5. The right to live in a system of free enterprise, free from compulsory labor, irresponsible private power, arbitrary public authority, and unregulated monopolies.

6. The right to come and go, to speak or be silent, free from spying of secret political police.

7. The right to equality before the law, with equal access to justice in fact.

8. The right to education, for work, for citizenship, and for personal growth and happiness.

9. The right to rest, recreation, and adventure; the opportunity to enjoy life and take part in an advancing civilization.

This and many other current vigorous restatements of our political ideas exhibits strikingly our leaders' belief in the people's capacity to redivert social trend. The actual redefinition of freedom marks a popular shift away from the individualistic Exploitive Tradition toward the social philosophy of the Great Tradition— further evidence that now is the moment in history to redesign and rebuild the social system!

II. Property Defined As "Function"

There is no clearer exhibit of the tendency for the social will to take charge of affairs than in the current trend in theory and practice of property ownership and administration. As the First Industrial Revolution ran its course, students of the culture saw that the definition of property as substance and of ownership as the right to withhold from use, was not only a violation of the American Way but was actually destroying the economic system itself by bringing more and more violent depressions and frightening mass unemployment.

The researches of the scholars and publicizers from Veblen and George and Bellamy to Brookings and Bassett Jones and James Feibleman,[3] prompted by the actual sequence of events, are slowly building the foundations of a positive and "realist" definition of property and its ownership. This point of view says that a thing is what it does, and what it can do; it consists of its possible as well as its actual uses. For example: an engine is defined as the "power it can produce" . . . A coal mine is "the useful work done by the energy released in the treatment of the coal" . . . A machine is "the goods and services that the people obtain from its operation." Thus while permitting, even encouraging private ownership, this view defines "things" in terms of their relations to the people generally; in terms of the contribution that the things can make to the good life of the larger group.

And thus once more we juxtapose the two rival traditions:

The Exploitive Tradition, with its individualistic, negative, substance, acquisitive, preëmptive, withholding-from-use emphasis.

The Great Tradition, with its social, positive, functional, development-for-use-of-the-people emphasis.

III . . . IV. THE GREAT TRADITION PRACTICES THE CONCEPTS OF EQUALITY AND COMMUNAL RELATIONSHIPS

Under the impetus of the American Declaration, the

[3] The reader should not miss James Feibleman's brilliant original analysis of this and other philosophical problems of democracy: *Positive Democracy* (University of North Carolina Press, 1940).

great charters of liberty of modern times have emphasized the concept of equality . . . "all men are created equal." Obviously, Mr. Jefferson and his colleagues did not mean that men were equal in height, strength, energy, wealth, mentality, sensitivity, ambition, greed, shrewdness—not in any physical, mental, or spiritual traits. The profound discussion of an "aristocracy of talents and virtue" of the author of The Declaration in his Virginia gubernatorial papers makes that very clear. He meant equality before the law . . . equality in sovereignty of personality . . . equality in the sense of dignity and worth of self, naturally, therefore, equality of opportunity for each individual to rise to the highest stature of which he is innately capable. This is clearly the intent of all the great declarations of man.

The spokesmen of the Great Tradition say it this way: At the center of a democratic society are two equal individuals, each of whose personalities is sovereign. Two sovereign personalities:

Each insisting on the integrity of his own self, but implicitly accepting the integrity of his neighbor. Each a believer in the validity of his own philosophy.

Each recognizing the necessity for frequent communion with others and the willing compromise which is sufficient to maintain happy relations with them.

Each fostering a way of living in which every man, woman, and child is free to grow to the finest possibilities that are in him.

Each whole-heartedly believing that a "man's a man for a' that," no matter what his property, skin color, race, nationality, or religion.

These two Persons have bound themselves together in a confederation; they rule equally together in a union which will free them by strengthening them. This is democracy according to the Great Tradition.

The Great Tradition maintains that the Individual can become a true Person only through the enhancing qualities of communion with other individuals. I am "Walt Whitman, a Kosmos, of Manhattan the son," sang the Poet. The individual steadily realizes his purpose and direction, dignity and value because in accelerating crescendo he senses the universal in his relatedness to the group, the community, the nation, mankind, and the universe—and this can come only by social communion. This is in opposition to the Exploitive Tradition which is completely individualistic . . . leaves no place for the individual's sensitivity for other individuals . . . denies equality of sovereignty of personality and rejects the dignity and worth of the individual. The most profound revelation of the Great Tradition, on the contrary, is its social nature . . . coöperative, not competitive . . . the "We" in place of the "I". As Waldo Frank puts it, it is this idea of social collaboration that leads one from the adolescent stage of culture development—like our own —in which the competitive individual is in the center, to the mature stage of the socialized and creative person. This stage is realized when the intuition of the Individual's organic connection with the cosmos inspirits his life with meaning and direction . . . when the intelligence of the people is "dedicated intrinsically . . . to the public welfare."

History abounds in evidence that creative man expresses himself profoundly when he is aware of the community; witness the great dams, the bridges, the new communities of today . . . the great cathedrals of the late Middle Ages. And it is now possible for America to make the greatest social reconstruction of all. By accepting the great social responsibility to lead in the rehabilitation of the world America can move into the greatest age of creative production in our history . . . can indeed reinstate the Great Tradition. The necessity of reading, discussing, studying about our participation day after day, month after month, in the coming years, will move us—in spite of ourselves—into the practice of the social thing.

Is this not the root to the great social religion which many philosophers have maintained we shall have to bring about on earth before the democratic idea will become an actuality?

V. The Great Tradition and Expression

The striking record of history discloses that western man has made two breath-taking achievements. He not only has designed and built great nations of communities and operated economic and political systems of bewildering complexity and gigantic power; he has, in addition, succeeded in stating his portrait of himself and his new culture in a great wealth of materials and media—community design, architecture, literature, music, painting, dance, theatre, what not—and he has done all this in such a way as to fuse technological efficiency with the principles of esthetics.

To do these things he was forced to devise profound ways of knowing, subtle methods of inquiry, and creative ways of working. Indeed, of all the striking achievements of modern man none is perhaps more signal than that of these very methods of portraying, appraising, and controlling his individual and social behavior. Taken in broad review, these ways of knowing and working vary greatly in nature and in relative effectiveness. For twenty-odd centuries philosophers have explored them, stated them in various forms, engaged in vigorous controversies about them. Each of the intellectual and emotional conflicts has added its bit of documented experience and hence of clarification. And perhaps of no creative period has that been more true than of our modern one, particularly the past century.

As a direct result of the brilliant achievement of our creative workers we have today at our command two subtle ways of working:

First—the method of intuition, always known to man and employed by speculative philosopher . . . technologist . . . artist . . . man-of-religion . . . scientist.
Second—the method of rational empiricism, of documentation, of experimental inquiry, of problem-solving thinking—also employed by man in these capacities.

TO CREATE "ORDER"

The modern man of the Great Tradition has always been above all, an "Orderer." Witness: He works his will upon a chaotic watershed and organizes it into a cultivated valley of farms and towns, with channels for production and distribution, transportation, communication, and markets. He transforms a wild hillside into a garden of beauty. His child naively organizes a roomful of scattered toys into a replica of human community. His engineers and technicians fuse a thousand mechanical metal parts into a unified self-propelled automobile. In the recurring episodes of western history leaders have appeared who have transformed political anarchy into order . . . rebuilt economic systems which have broken down . . . stated the mood and the mind of the people in poems, songs, plays, paintings, dances. The creative task has always been the same—to reduce a miscellany to order, to transform unrelated elements into an organization. Western man has never shown his powers of abstraction more effectively than in these achievements of organization.

As we confront the task of redesigning and reconstructing a badly battered society, we see that this creative capacity of organization has never been needed more critically than today. Fortunately our fathers in building both the structure of our society and the battering rams of its destruction, have also passed on to us the means of its reconstruction. Through hundreds of years of creative effort they developed these two efficient and beautiful methods of work—the documenting techniques of man-as-scientist and the intuitive methods of man-as-artist. These are both powerful and indispensable instruments for organization and reducing a bewilderingly chaotic miscellany of peoples and broken states to order.

Our America—greatest stronghold of physical as well as spiritual power on the earth today—has now become the secure haven for a vast concentration of the western world's creative imagination and design. Here is the world's fulcrum of creative reconstruction; now is the favored moment to provide a world faced by anarchy with the concepts of order and design; here is an army of creative men and women trained and experienced in the use of the two great methods of work. No bombing of cities, no burning of the books, no destruction of the house, the literature, the music, the theatre, the community of mankind can destroy these creative instruments. Nothing short of the mass murder of the sensitive, talented men and women of the entire earth could accomplish that!

It becomes of great importance therefore for our people to understand these two methods of work and their possibilities. First the "scientific" one.

I. The Scientific Method of Discovering and Producing Order

Instruments for Organizing Thought and Feeling

The foundation of a technically efficient civilization was prepared in the thousand years between the settling down of the European tribes and the completion of the first modern nation-states. During that time the five great instruments by which western man was able to put together his power-machine industrialism and his "democracy" were developed. The first of these was a group of languages which facilitated enormously man's ability to see relationships and organize thought and feeling. Out of the nine major divisions of the language map of the world [4] one, the Indo-European, spreading out from the Caspian Sea to India on the east and to the British Isles on the west, merged later with Europe's Latin and developed into a score and a half of closely related national languages which have become the means of communication for three-quarters of the inhabitants of the globe.

[4] The Indo-European, the Semitic, the Hamitic, the one-syllable languages of China and Asia, the Euro-Altaic, the Dravidian, the Malayan, the Polynesian, the Bantu.

I refer to the obvious fact of these modern languages because without them the modern methods of science, of machine technology, of business organization, and of social coöperation could not have come into existence.

Through these multi-word and multi-meaning languages (each one composed of thirty-odd thousand words with the capacity of conveying millions of meanings) the Europeans created subtle instruments of analytic thought and organization. An organization is an integration—an organized whole—of related elements; it is at the bottom discerning and stating relationships. This mastery of the concept of relationship distinguishes modern man from primitive or early civilized man more definitely than any other single factor. Creative individuals of the Great Tradition, prying into the action of heavenly bodies, of plant, animal, and human life, asked millions of times, "Why, when that happens, does that other thing happen also?" "Why do things seem to change together?" "Why, this ever-recurring ordered relationship?"

The special significance of western man's success in developing the modern languages is that the creative invention of measuring instruments, the method of scientific inquiry itself could not advance without the antecedent linguistic means of thought and understanding. What was needed, we can see now, was a body of intellectual and emotional instruments through which ordered meanings could be perceived and stated; instruments which, above all, would state relationships. Without the conceptual and organizing thinking made possible by linguistic means, the scientist could not perceive regularities in apparent chance-like arrangements, and the artist could not create an adequate organization out of the miscellany of the earth.

✓ ✓ ✓

As their curiosity grew, our scientists and technologists of the Great Tradition developed the concepts for another body of subtle instruments of abstract thinking: measurement . . . scale . . . equal unit . . . zero point. Without these and the astounding measuring advances of our own times, we could not have either the efficient machine technology, or the relatively precise knowledge of the physical universe which is now ours. Indeed every process, every mechanical thing in our modern civilization depends upon the science and technology of measurement; for example, the mapping and sounding of the seas, the mapping of the extent and height of the land masses of the earth . . . the temporal sequence of events and their geographic location . . . the engines and machines of modern industry . . . the production and transmission of giant power and its decentralized use in workable small units . . . heavier-than-air flying machines, self-propelled land vehicles and the instantaneous electrical transmission of words, tones, and sounds around the earth. The achievements themselves are obvious; I refer to them because of their significance in the understanding and control of the environment, and as a revelation of the creative capacity of the talented members of our civilization.

The invention and use of the instruments piled up mountains of "measured facts," created an insistent need for organizing these data, and this led to the clarification of new concepts—"rank order" . . . "standardization" —concepts that deal with *relationship* and hence with order. In fact out of the invention of scales and units and their hectic application has developed the practice of the "rank ordering" of individuals, their personal and social development, performance, and achievement. Indeed, our egocentric, competitive society has tended to become, not only a standardized but a "rank order" civilization as well—witness its awards, prizes, graduations, degrees, and the like.

Thus we see measuring devices also as instruments to expedite psychological organization. And here is an object lesson of great importance for the social scientist as well as for the practical statement; control of the economic-political-social order may wait upon the same two steps that developed industrial civilization—namely, the invention of measuring instruments and the clarification of ideas through the ordering and standardizing of meaning.

↗ ↗ ↗

But it was in the perfection of the higher mathematics, especially after the incredible seventeenth century that the modern Europeans succeeded in creating the most powerful instrument for the detection and the statement of relationship and hence for the discovery of order as shown by scientific "law." In a "century of genius" a galaxy of creative mathematicians—Galileo, Newton, Descartes, and Huygens, to name the most famous quadrumvirate—produced one of the two most original creations of the human spirit. This was the astounding mathematical instrument of thinking called in academic terms, the algebra . . . the algebraic, trigonometrical, and logarithmic functions . . . the analytic geometry . . . the calculus. The invention of these made it possible for the first time to sort out the chaotic tangle of observations of the physical world into a series of clear, ordered generalizations. Hence the psychological importance of this creative achievement: here was a tool of clear meaning and understanding.

This brief reference to the achievement of the mathematical masters of abstract thought will remind us that creative talent had to be devoted to the development of instruments of thinking before their application could come about in the perfection of machine technology. But the mathematical instruments for stating relationships between forces were devised and these helped to make it possible to discover such hidden principles as those of electro-magnetism and of the basic ideas underlying the prime mover and the modern manipulative machine. The technological result today is the efficient and beautiful straight-line factory system of sequential production, the integration of workers, departments, industries, assembly lines. The total human result is that today we stand on the verge of physical abundance for the first time in history.

✔ ✔ ✔

Recurringly we cross the deepening trail of western man's search for order. In the seventeenth century under the leadership of Francis Bacon, René Descartes, and such organizations as the Royal Society of England and its College of Fellows (witness—Newton, Boyle, Wren, Cowley, and Samuel Pepys) the cumulations of measured observations were sorted out into the first systematic organized categories which have come to be called the sciences. The search for order resulted eventually in a synthesis of ways of observing and of treating observations, of thinking and of the accompanying attitudes that, taken together have come to be known among the scientists as the scientific method . . . and among the pragmatic philosophers who made the most profound verbal descriptions of it, as the experimental mode of inquiry.

Its beginning and its end points are one and the same —the hypothesis; this is the statement of the clearest relationship that can be drawn from the generalization of the known data. The end point is regarded as tentatively accepted "law"—which in itself is also hypothesis, to be held with an open mind, with a view to its modification as instruments of observation and measurement, of mathematical treatment, and of the art of thinking itself, become more precise, more discerning. Between the beginning and end points of hypothesis are the steps of the scientific method—observation with instruments of measurement, experiments to test the truth of the hypothesis . . . their systematic classification and tabulation with the aid of standardized frequency distributions of equal intervals . . . tentative inferences called "principles" or even "law"—actually new hypotheses.

These steps, taken together, constitute the scientific method of inquiry. This art of concept-making is the result of the improvement of methods of human work begun three hundred years ago by the philosophical discussions of Bacon's *Advancement of Learning* and Descartes' *Discourse on Method* and brought to its highest point in our time by a new generation of philosophers from Charles Peirce (1839–1914) to John Dewey (1859–). Here is the pragmatic interpretation of meaning and truth which emphasizes the biosocial-evolutionary process . . . life is seen as a succession of problem situations, blocked activities, uncertainties. Here the brave new life in a brave new world is regarded deliberately as precarious, problematic, preparatory; experimental thinking is studied as "problem solving" and ideas are verified by the test of actual consequences.

✓   ✓   ✓

Here then is the end point of centuries of exciting mental discoveries in a line of development by which men came to think things out for themselves instead of accepting things by the authority of others. It cannot be questioned that these concepts of the pragmatic climate of opinion made possible the physical industrial civilization. Moreover, it also produced the stuff of the concepts of relationship and organization which have now become the nub of the whole "realist" interpretation of man, society, and the universe. This has been grasped in our day by scientists and artists working in every medium of expression, as the most profound idea of modern times. It appears in the concept of "law" of the scientist . . . as the "organic form" of the whole expressionist movement in architecture, industrial design, the graphic and plastic arts, the theatre arts, literary expression. It appears as the "functionality" of mathematics and of the arts. The new psychologies, "realist" philosophy, positive rather than negative democracy, as well as the new social and physical engineering, all emphasize this idea of "relationship."

From the day of Newton, Leibnitz, and El Greco to the current one of deForrest, Einstein, and Wright excited explorers on a half dozen widely separated creative frontiers have come to perceive and to state successfully in some area of human life this great concept of relational organization.

✓ ✓ ✓

Thus, out of the creative ordeal of the men of science in the Great Tradition, we today have inherited five instruments of precise thought by which we can produce a degree of order in our disorganized world. These are, we repeat:

—languages of great complexity and subtle power of meaning,
—concepts and instruments of more precise measurement,
—mathematical methods of detecting and stating relationships,
—the concept and process of scientific method, of inquiry, and of work,
—institutions for creative research and the dissemination of ideas.

These can be more compactly phrased as two: (1) languages capable of precise conceptualizing and generalizing statement . . . (2) the scientific method of inquiry and work. These are the distinctive "intellectual" contributions of the Great Tradition; these made it possible for western man to preëmpt, clear, settle, and exploit the earth, to bring mankind in the middle twentieth century to the threshold of physical and spiritual abundance.

But there was another mood . . . another concept . . . another method of inquiry and way of working.

II. THE INTUITIVE METHOD OF PRODUCING ORDER

How, do you think, did men build Karnak . . . the Parthenon . . . the temples of Amerindia . . . the Taj Mahal . . . the Gothic Cathedrals? How did they speak the Sermon on the Mount . . . write the *Iliad* . . . the books of Confucius . . . the *Divine Comedy?* How did they paint the dome of the Sistine Chapel?

These are all works of Order . . . of profound organization. The human creators of these masterpieces of design must have had a sensitive and effective instrument and a universal method of working to appraise, understand, design, and construct in a way to satisfy men throughout a hundred generations.

They did. Long before men could measure and "rank-order" things and people with precise, mechanical instruments on scales of equal units; long before they could plot coördinated data, detect points of inflection on curves for which equations had been written, they had both a sensitive instrument and an acute method of design and construction.

These were ancient and they were efficient even if they did not employ the paraphernalia of "science." The method was a combination of thinking and feeling that for centuries has been badly named "intuition." The instrument was that fusion of body, mind, and spirit that today we call the organism; as the new psychology puts it, "the organism-acting-as-a-whole." It has been sponsored for many centuries by a heterogeneous company including scientists, speculative philosophers, poets, novelists, critics, social engineers, students of society, musicians, dancers, playwrights, painters, sculptors, industrial designers. Irrespective of his chosen medium each one works as "artist," as imaginative worker, molding a mis-·cellany of materials into the one best organization which will state his own unique view of life and the world.

It is badly named "intuition," I say, because that term carries with most people a transcendental, supernatural meaning. It cannot be insisted too strongly, however, that this concept and organic process is not "mystic" in any supernatural sense; on the contrary, it is founded on two generations of research in endocrinology, neurology, physiology, on the work of half a dozen schools of psychology and on the independent generalizations of the artists who use the very method of organic awareness in all fields of expression. And—it assumes and is founded upon a scientific, naturalistic outlook.

Many of those who recognize the intuitive approach think of it as sometimes orienting and guiding and sometimes supplementing the so-called rational or experimental approach. They feel, however, that the experimental approach depends too exclusively on the verbal and analytic description of the report of the five senses to be depended upon as a sole method. While agreeing that the world cannot be properly understood or controlled if the reports of the senses are neglected, they insist that used alone they are not sufficient even to set a problem. As Waldo Frank has stated it:

Reality must be apprehended before the report of the senses can *make* sense . . . a prehension (to use Whitehead's word) must infuse *the entire process of experience*, qualitatively giving it life. This prehension is not transcendental in the cant meaning of supernatural or supersensory; it is simply the method of awareness of the organism as a whole. Its best name is the intuition . . . The true intuition, having the whole man as its organ, includes the reports of the senses and what is rationally induced from them. But the intuition's immediate quality is as different from these reports as a life is different from its chemic elements.[5]

Let us pay close attention to the concept stated here; namely that the total organism's response, if not shunted off into side tangents by the too tense concentration on rational analysis, will apprehend reality, and in doing so will make use of the reports of the senses. Note again Frank's last sentence: "The intuition's immediate quality is as different from these reports [of the separate senses] as a life is different from its chemic elements."

Although probably older than the scientific outlook, the intuitive outlook is less clearly defined, even to this day. Throughout the recent centuries especially, professional philosophers devoted themselves to it less vigorously than to the experimental method of inquiry. Artists themselves have been content to state their views of life in their respective media of expression without trying to make their methods of work articulate. Hence the basic concepts of the intuitive approach have emerged with less definitiveness.

But, in our own day, students in the sciences and the arts have revived and extended the study of the intuitive process. Philosophers and scientists are describing how they work and their descriptions and analyses of their own "creative acts" confirm the findings of the artists and the men of religion with regard to the intuitive approach. Laboratory scientists tell me that the verbal ana-

[5] Waldo Frank: "Our Guilt in Fascism," *The New Republic*, May 6, 1940, p. 605.

lytic description of the reports of the independent senses are indispensable, but that they cannot be depended upon alone. I am convinced from their reports that the drawing of "scientific hypotheses" is carried in the same intuitive, organismic way employed by "artists." Especially do the scientific men agree with Whitehead and Frank in stressing the role of feeling in the rising of the "prehension" and the danger of the too-tense concentration on the direct confrontation and analysis of alternatives according to the pragmatic analysis of problem solving. They agree that this tense concentration upon the so-called "problem" tends to shut off immediate needed meanings. The whole process must be one of relaxed organic approach. Instead of confronting the problem too tensely and directly—*a la* the Dewey problem-solving analysis—it is as if one were looking at the problem from the side. Flashes of insight appear to come as from a tangent when one is relaxed. We let down our guards . . . let the problem creep up on us . . . let it "take" us by a tangential, associational approach, the organism-as-a-whole approaching the situation by a kind of emotional "flank attack."

Thus, Man-the-Abstractionist . . . Man-the-Orderer has created two methods of organization—the method of Intuition or Organic Awareness and the method of Experimental Inquiry. Both are necessary if our chaotic world is to be put together again. Both are the methods and instruments of Expression in the Great Tradition.

A few sensitive souls throughout western history have given themselves to the creative ordeal of using them to state the Great Tradition. Some, in their respective centuries, learned to utter that tradition in laws, in profound judicial decisions, in great state papers. Others preached it through modern forms of social religion. Some carved it out of stone and molded it in plaster. Others hymned it in words, rhymed it and sang it or danced it with the body. And some built it through the educated lives of their protégés in school.

But all sang the song: There are. unnumbered Supremes . . . We shall rule together.

Taken altogether, it was they who made clearer and more beautiful the practical administration of the great constellation of ideas—the Supreme Value of the Individual. It was they who have doggedly sought to transform the competitive Individualist into the communal Person.

The evidence is all about us that the Americans are now mustering these two great methods of inquiry and work. This is the gaint leverage that, energized by the fusion of deep disinterested sense of humanity and of enlightened self-interest, will make the gesture that will literally move the social world.

Now is the moment.

We Must Speak of the Peace

You tell me, warning, that this is war
. . . that I am not to speak of the peace.

I tell you we are speaking of the peace.
We design the peace now as the only guarantee of win-
ning the war.

I tell you there are two wars, two fascisms
. . . and the two are one,
tomorrow's war at home,
today's war abroad.
To speak of the peace now, is to win the war,
—the two wars . . .
tomorrow's war at home,
as well as today's war abroad.

You ask me,
suppose we win the war,
what then?
Can we win the peace?

I tell you we are winning the peace now,
Every victory and every set-back, now,
Is a campaign in tomorrow's war at home.

So I tell you we must speak of the peace,
Even while we war.

Five

WHAT THEY MEAN BY "WINNING THE PEACE"

A House Divided Against Itself

What does it mean—"to win the peace"? The phrase is on the lips of thousands of vocal Americans who are discussing the War and the Peace, but it means different things to different men. American leadership, like that of every industrial country, is a house divided against itself. A fierce struggle for political power, which has been under way for a decade and a half, is sharpening the cleavage. Recognizing that now or never in our time is the moment to win Tomorrow's war at home hundreds of spokesmen as far apart as extreme Right from farthest Left are speaking out vigorously.

CENTER-TO-RIGHT *vs.* CENTER-TO-LEFT

But the line-up, scattered over a wide range though it is, already sets a cohesive Center-to-Right against a gathering Center-to-Left. Although the two differ internally on details of strategy and tactics, each side is quite clear on what it wants from the social system. In general, the Center-to-Right believes in the Exploitive Tradition . . .

111

freedom interpreted as minimum restraint . . . every man for himself and every country for itself and not much participation in world affairs—in short, in varying degrees of pre-depression, pre-war *status quo*. The Center-to-Left, however, believes in the Great Tradition . . . that we must design programs of national and world-wide social reconstruction to fit the historical conclusions drawn from the moving trends . . . that we'll never go back to anything pre-depression or pre-war . . . and concludes, with Henry Wallace, that we are in an actual "People's Revolution" and that now is the moment to guarantee our children a free world.

Within each side there are considerable differences—from the middlish-near-the-Center to an extremist Right or Left. Among the extreme Right, for example, are the utter die-hards—the America Firsters, the freedom-without-restraint business enterprisers, actually some former collaborators of Franco Spain, Fascist Italy, and Nazi Germany—their names are well known. Confronted by international problems, they are for an isolated, debt-collecting, tariff-raising United States. For the coming war at home they are now preparing an all-out attack upon the New Deal agencies of social control. They are for "taking the brakes off of business," for a return to an uncontrolled free enterprise by free competition in a free market. They recommend, as does the Hearst press, for example: "an armed, quasi-democracy."

Between these utter reactionaries of the extreme Right and the center is an heterogeneous group of business leaders and politicians who grant that marked social change is a fact, that some modification must be made in the economic-social system to fit it, and that some American participation in world leadership is necessary. They prefer modified imperialism and free-market regime under Anglo-Saxon direction and control, granting Russia and China limited participation. In this Right-to-near-center group we find support for feeding, hospitalizing, and policing the harassed regions of the world at the close of the war, and a begrudging acceptance of the need for minor regulative controls on the domestic economic system.

Differences within the Center-to-Left are marked out equally clearly—at the extreme Left stand the die-hards of Communism and Socialism, some of whom—until Pearl Harbor—got themselves into close collaboration with the die-hard Right. With the exception of this extremist faction, the body of the Center-to-Left follows the leadership of the Henry Wallace wing of the New Deal government. These are for active collaboration with Britain, Russia, China, and the smaller members of the United Nations in the joint humane reconstruction of an anarchic post-war world . . . for cancelling world debts and for free trade . . . for giving away billions in food, raw materials, and commodities to start the national economic systems of the world going again . . . and for keeping the domestic economic system running at full employment without regard to the bookkeeping "costs." In short, the Center-to-Left has the capacity to instate the Great Tradition.

To distinguish so sharply the Center-to-Right from the Center-to-Left, I am told, is a "divisive" move that will destroy our unity, oppose the possibility of cooperation. On the contrary, this separating out of allies and opponents organizes the kaleidoscope of events into startlingly meaningful patterns, it clarifies issues and stimulates thought. It enables those less experienced in the analysis of social trend to read signs that formerly were intelligible only to professional students. It serves to coalesce that great nucleus of the population that under the compulsion of terrible danger will seek solidarity in taking thought together, in the prompt discovery of solutions for our problems, and in the swift design and operation of programs of action. The enemies of a decent world are being named and pushed out into the limelight of publicity, and allies foregather; they know now with whom and against whom they must fight. It prepares our men and women to assume the role of Answerers in a world of defeatism and doubt. Far from being a divisive move, this clarification of our personnel and of our task energizes America's muscles from hitherto unused reservoirs of creative power.

The Line-Up

Let these two groups of Americans speak their minds then. Let them tell what they mean when they say "win the peace."

I. The Center-to-Left Speaks

We begin with our President. In his message to the 77th Congress, January 6, 1941, Mr. Roosevelt said: "In the future days, which we seek to make secure, we look to a world founded upon four essential human freedoms." The first two are the long established freedoms of speech and worship, the third and fourth, however, are new to charters of liberty, so I quote them in full:

The third is freedom from want—which, translated into world terms, means economic understandings which will secure to every nation a healthy peace-time life for its inhabitants—everywhere in the world.

The fourth is freedom from fear—which, translated into world terms, means a world-wide reduction of armaments to such a point and in such a thorough fashion that no nation will be in a position to commit an act of physical aggression against any neighbor—anywhere.

From the most powerful sounding board in the democratic world—the American presidency—comes the pronouncement that America fights for a disarmed world of economic abundance.

Mr. Roosevelt's associates are putting his general doctrine into historical perspective, supplying more detailed specifications. We are in the midst of a long-running People's Revolution . . . this is the Century of the Common Man . . . we must feel with new attitudes and think with new ideas that will outlaw mental conservatism. I quote them:

THE PEOPLE'S REVOLUTION

Vice-President Wallace, addressing the Free World Association on May 8, 1942, matched President Roosevelt's Four Freedoms with Four Duties:

The duty to produce to the limit,
The duty to transport as rapidly as possible to the field of battle,
The duty to fight with all that is within us,
The duty to build a peace—just, charitable, and enduring.

It is the fourth duty "which inspires the other three . . . as we move forward toward the Four Freedoms of this people's revolution . . . We failed in our job after World War I, we did not know how to go about it to build an enduring world-wide peace . . . we did not build a peace treaty on the fundamental doctrine of the people's revolution." But having learned much from our errors, Mr. Wallace said, we can now win a war on every home front—and that is nothing less than a revolution. He implements Mr. Roosevelt's Third Freedom: "When we begin to think about the significance of freedom from want for the average man, then we know the revolution of the past 150 years has not been completed, either here in the United States or in any other nation in the world. We know that this revolution cannot stop until freedom from want has actually been attained." This is followed by the kind of specifics that the common man wants to hear from his political leaders: We have the resources, and this is our moment to use them to win the people's revolution.

Modern science, which is a by product and an essential part of the people's revolution, has made it technologically possible to see that all of the people of the world get enough to eat. Half in fun and half seriously, I said the other day to Madame Litvinoff: 'The object of this war is to make sure that everybody in the world has the privilege of drinking a quart of milk a day.' She replied, 'Yes, even a pint.' The peace must mean a better standard of living for the common man, not merely in the United States and England but also in India, Russia, China, and Latin America—not merely in the United Nations, but also in Germany and Italy and Japan.

A month later in another speech, Mr. Wallace made America's world leadership in winning the peace even clearer:

America is building up in the full sun of a new day for a peace which is not based on imperialistic intervention. The American peace, the peace of the common man, must be translated into freedom everywhere. America will not have made her contribution until 90 per cent of the adults of the world can read and write, until all the children of the world can have at least a pint of milk a day, until education brings with it such a sensitive responsibility that all the people of the world can be trusted to take part in democratic government.

Mr. Milo Perkins, Mr. Wallace's associate on and the executive director of the federal Board of Economic Warfare, also accepts the historian's interpretation of a "people's revolution" covering centuries:

This is a long, long fight to make a mass-production economy work. The battle started when machines became important in the lives of men. It should be over within the generation following this conflict. The battle will be won when we have built up mass-consumption to a point where markets can absorb the output of our mass-production industries running at top speed.

This leading official also commits his government to running the economic system at full employment load in peace as well as in war:

The plain people of this earth know what they want in the post-war period. Above all else they want to be *wanted;* they want a chance to work and be useful. They want an income which will give them enough food and clothing and shelter and medical care to drive the fear of want from the family fire side . . . The plain people will be understanding about the problems of readjustment. They will work hard for all this and they will walk any reasonable roads to these ends. But the chains of the ages have snapped. The one thing they won't do is to take 'no' for a final answer to their cry for full employment. Not after all this suffering; not when they see themselves surrounded later on by too much of what they need most and yet might not be able to get.

That is the voice of dynamic political leadership, a successful business man putting his mind and heart and courage to work in what he and his leader Henry Wallace say bluntly, is "the people's revolution" in "the century of the common man."

Secretary of the Interior Ickes, on June 21, 1942, backed up the Roosevelt-Wallace-Perkins stand that the post-war period shall really become "the People's Century" . . . "We are entering the century of the common man; the free nations will determine that it must be controlled by the common man."

Our No. 1 war production man—Mr. Donald M. Nelson, in his first statement on the post-war outlook, June 9, 1942, also declared that Mr. Roosevelt's "Freedom from Want" can become a reality for the entire world.

For a generation we have been living on the edge of a new world; we are only now beginning to realize it. For the first time in the history of the human race there can be enough of everything to go around. Poverty is not inevitable any more. The sum total of the world's greatest possible output of goods divided by the sum total of the world's inhabitants no longer means a little less than enough for everybody . . . We shall have the most magnificent opportunity any nation ever had. To accept that opportunity we need only to have the good pioneer sense not to be frightened by it just because it calls for new mental attitudes and new habits of thought.

Thus an expert in business blue printed the government experts' idea of the people's revolution. Mr. Nelson said that the profit motive, while still a key factor, is no longer the main spring of our economic life, if we are to banish poverty, we must carry over into the post-war period the attitude that has characterized our war production drive, that "outlaws mental conservatism."

Speaking as our Ambassador to Great Britain, Mr. John G. Winant, committed the United Nations to a war against poverty, sickness, and unemployment: "We must move on to a great social offensive if we are to win the war completely." Fascism, he said, came from poverty and unemployment and "to crush Fascism at its roots we must crush depression." And we can do it:

We have enough technical knowledge and organizing ability to respond to this awakening of the social conscience. We have enough courage. We must put it to use. When the war is done the drive for tanks must become a drive for houses. The drive for food to prevent the enemy from starving us must become a drive for food to satisfy the needs of all the people in all countries. The drive for physical fitness in the forces must become a drive for bringing the death and sickness rates in the whole population down to the lowest possible level. The drive for manpower in war must become a drive for employment to make freedom from want a living reality.

What winning the peace means to the government's National Resources Planning Board is shown by their implementation of President Roosevelt's Four Freedoms with the Board's New Bill of Rights, previously referred to (see p. 60). Charles W. Eliot, the Director, recently said:

We are not going back to anything. We are going forward. We could not stop the march of progress if we wanted, but we can do something about the direction of the changes that will follow victory. For that reason we propose to plan ahead . . .

To make progress in that direction . . . the thoughts of a democratic people need rallying cries, or slogans. We who work with the National Resources Planning Board are using three slogans in relation to post-war planning: full employment, security and upbuilding America . . . People in Washington say that 'when the whistle blows,' meaning when the war is over, will be time enough to think how we shall go about providing these things. But perhaps you have the same sneaking suspicion that comes to me sometimes—that there won't be any whistle this time . . . It may very well be that the chaos which follows the downfalls of the Japs, the Fascists and the Nazis will be almost indistinguishable from war.

Prominent business men both in and outside of government reveal a new attitude about the fact of social change and the necessity of new minds and new programs to fit the new day. Mr. W. M. Kiplinger, for years one of America's leading business reporters, analysts, and interpreters, says in his book *Washington Is Like That* that the United States will have to take the lead in reviving a ravaged post-war world.

You can get the general idea if you think in terms of a world Reconstruction Finance Corporation and a mammoth Works Progress Administration Program. When the war is over, the United States government will be the biggest of big businesses and this is a new phenomenon, for after the last war there was no strong central government. Now there is and the people, with their votes, will compel their strong central government to do whatever is necessary to run the economy at full blast . . . Washington will force business men to think in terms of the total economy, and learn some of the lessons taught by the graduate schools.

Labor union leaders, he says, will play a part also, more of them being drawn into government, both during the war and afterward. "They will help decide broad policies of industry, working through government committees, to a greater extent after the war." Mr. Kiplinger reports that post-war plans call for jobs for all "even if the government must make the jobs." As for the budget, it will not be balanced for many years. "A public debt of $150,000,000,000 is indicated. Planners say it doesn't hurt so long as we don't try to pay it off."

To point out the widespread expression of the Center-to-Left position on what it means to "win the peace," I have quoted distinguished leaders of politics and business rather than individuals and groups traditionally known as the Liberal Left. Although hundreds of the latter could be quoted, I am confident that we need not multiply quotations. What the Center-to-Left wants is clear—the coöperation of government, industry, business, farmers, and professionals to put the New Bill of Rights—largely an economic bill—into actual going operation coördinate and in full force with the civil and political bill of rights established in the last two centuries. That's what the People's Revolution of Mr. Wallace *et al.* means. It certainly does not mean the all-out adoption of any Ism—neither communism nor socialism. It means the continuation and extension of the American Way of regulating "I" and, wherever necessary, of interjecting "We" into the social system to stimulate as well as to control "I".

II. The Center-to-Right Speaks

Because I find no common ground of either intelligent discussion or practicable political union with the extreme die-hards of the Center-to-Right I shall not use valuable space to quote many of them. What the extreme Right means by "winning the peace" is shown very clearly by the activity of the Joint Congressional Economy Committee (including such men as Byrd, George, McKellar, Nye, Woodrum, Tabor, Doughton, and Howard W. Smith). It means, straight out, the reinstatement after the war of the Exploitive Tradition, the reëstablishment of the economic order current in the industrial countries before the depression of 1929-1939. Witness their unflagging efforts to destroy the enterprises of the government: the abolition of the National Youth Administration, the Civilian Conservation Corps, the Farm Security Administration, and the Works Progress Administration . . . the curtailment of the activities of the Surplus Marketing Administration . . . the undermining of America's war efficiency by the curtailment of the Tennessee Valley Authority and other national power developments.

Mr. Alfred M. Landon, Republican presidential nominee in 1936, speaking June 14, 1942 before an Elks

Lodge Flag Day Meeting, warned against discussing the peace while the war continued: it was "futile and dangerous . . . the peace will not be of our sole devising, for we have partners." He declared that it was "both unnecessary and dangerous" for our leaders to build up hopes of a utopian world in the future. "There are no grounds for such utopian hopes," taking a position as the exact opposite of the scale from Messrs. Wallace, Perkins, and Nelson.

The Ku Klux Klan, through its Imperial Wizard, J. A. Colescott, also subscribes to the Landon view: "It is disturbing and dangerous for individuals and groups to talk of international unions after the war or of who will write the peace terms . . . etc. There is nothing to be gained, but much to be lost, by the injection of post-war questions at this time."

The President of Harvard University, Dr. James B. Conant, joins in attacking the notion that a world much better than we now have can be built after the war. Deploring the full-production-at-full-employment kind of economic system as a "utopian" one, he blamed its failure on those who during the past twenty years had tried to bring in a better world: "No small measure of blame must be laid at the door of the prevalent utopian philosophy . . . surely the history of the United States from 1917 to 1941 shows how the utopian philosophy would defeat the very movements it would foster . . . I am no defeatist as to human hopes . . . [but] to my mind the Utopians who foresee the future in terms of a world made perfect by technology and the applied social sciences . . . are equally mistaken. The facts of history and of human nature to me speak of a universe constructed on totally different principles. The problem of evil seems to be as ever-present as the air we breathe."

The industrialist-business men of the extreme Right leave no doubt as to their position. They bluntly assume that it is impossible to run a free enterprise system without depressions: "Our plans should clearly allow for a business slump when the war is over . . . the transition back to peace-time production must involve an interlude of unemployment and depression." [1] Furthermore the economic measures of the New Deal are dismissed as "a lot of nonsense," and the hope is expressed that "we shall return in the post-war period to some old-fashioned remedies."

Most of the members of *Fortune*'s Tenth Round Table "On Demobilizing the War Economy," September 5-7, 1941, were skeptical of the need for making changes in the social system after the war. The Editors' published report *After the War—What* deals with the problem of "what to do with 10,000,000 new workers and a tremendously expanded plant when the emergency ends," and insists that "the time to plan is *now*."

The report of the majority bloc grants "that circumstances today are different" and "modern technological warfare imposes far more of a burden on economic life than did the war twenty-five years ago," and seems to regret what it calls "the prevalent defeatism today as to the economic aftermath of this war." The Center-to-

---

[1] Murray Shields: *Post-War Economic Prospects*, published under the imprint of the National Association of Manufacturers, 1941.

Left's insistence on running the economic system at full employment after the war is called "defeatism" by the majority who say: "In principle we are opposed to government operation of war-time plant for peace-time purposes . . . new inventions in industry should arise to create peace-time jobs." Against this view the liberal minority urges "government, after the war, to operate plants in certain industries, such as aluminum, in order to maintain a yardstick."

The majority see no need for making drastic changes to get what Messrs. Wallace, Perkins, Nelson, Eliot, Hansen, Soule, *et al.* demand—namely, running the economic system at full employment. They will be satisfied if the government extends war orders for six months after the armistice, tapering them off, and making sure of "some form of dismissal wage to tide the worker over until he finds a new job, thus reducing the need for post-war relief expenditures. The Round Table members grant that "certain public works will be essential for social reasons" but they are convinced that the backlog of shortages must be given an opportunity to absorb defense workers in the post-war period "*before* any large scale public works program for that purpose is put into effect." [2] They insist that "the greatest single outlet for post-war investment and employment lies in housing and urban reconstruction . . . While we believe in a government program for slum clearance, the main housing job can be done only by private enterprise." The point of

[2] On this point a minority report, submitted by liberal labor leaders and economists, said that they favored "a vastly expanded social security system in the post-war period, financed much more than at present from general national income, that is, from taxes on ability to pay."

view is summed up well by: "We believe that our standard of living can best be advanced and our democracy
maintained after the war by the widest dispersion of initiative, rather than its centralized control by either government or monopolistic groups . . . Responsibility for
planning and operation of business must remain with
management. However, it would be very helpful if labor
leaders would educate labor in the understanding of the
proper workings of the American industrial system."
Their conception of the proper role of the United States
in a world economic system is shown by their statement:
"We should accept the responsibility of being the world's
leading creditor nation, organize long term foreign
financing, currency stabilization, lower trade barriers."

I have quoted the majority bloc of *Fortune*'s Tenth
Round Table at some length because it epitomizes best of
all the position of the business element of the Center-to-
Right.

Mr. Thomas E. Dewey, runner-up for the Republican
presidential nomination in 1940 and elected Governor of New York in 1942, is an example of the Center-to-
Right leadership—near the Center—which has accepted
some of the concepts and outcomes of "planning." While
admitting that economic planning will be necessary after
the war, he said it must be undertaken by people "who
believe in and understand both American workers and
business men"—meaning the Center-to-Right leadership.
At a speech to the Bond Club in New York City, Mr.
Dewey said that industrialists and business men had
shown their genius by passing a miracle of production to
give the armed forces the tools with which to win the

war. He warned vigorously, these same geniuses must begin to do their own planning against the end of the war; otherwise "the little collectivist planners will surely be here to take over the job because they are doing it now." We must be prepared to avert a future dedicated to a "creeping collectivism."

But this does not mean that we should go back to *laissez-faire:* Mr. Dewey rejected that philosophy and accepted the idea that the governmental controls that emerge from the war cannot be entirely abandoned. He has moved with the times in other respects as shown by his assumption that the war debts should be cancelled and that we would have to "lease-lend or give away—and I favor mostly giving away—both to our allies and defeated enemies, food, medical aid, machinery, and equipment to rehabilitate their destitute people and rebuild their bomb-torn lands." But, he warns, "we cannot establish a sound post-war economy, beyond the first period of emergency reconstruction, on any basis of international charity. We must find means of exchanging with other nations the things they can use and the things we can use." And he strongly advised industrialists to cooperate in "seeking ways and means to keep production rolling after the war."

Former President Herbert Hoover and his co-author, the international negotiator, Hugh Gibson, in their new book, *The Problems of Lasting Peace,* also show the influence of changing social trends on neo-Victorian orientations. Even though their historical analysis is superficial and over-simplified, we have here a good view of typical American rightish points of view that are being modified by current devastating world trends. They accept "American responsibility for vast gifts to rehabilitation . . . the writing off of inter-governmental loans and reparations as uncollectible . . . the impossibility of a Pax Americana . . . the feeding and rehabilitation of the warring peoples to avoid chaos and pestilence." But nevertheless they stand with the Center-to-Right, advocating a free economy in the international economic field.

Even the great world newspaper, the *New York Times*, known traditionally for its position near the Center, has publicly announced its conviction that the world is moving into a new way of life:

We are on the eve of a new way of life. Your future is going to be altered profoundly . . . the house you live in, your method of doing business, your social life, your relation with labor or capital, are about to take on new forms . . . real estate will finally take on new life, building will finally achieve a modern form, factories will finally emerge from slums, the cost of distributing goods will finally begin to decrease.

What They Mean when They Speak of the Peace

There is a discernible tendency for spokesmen nearer the Center—both of the Right and the Left—to search for certain possible common bases for a better national program after the war. With the exception of the most adamant isolationists and die-hard free enterprisers, both sides are aware that social change has moved so far that there is no possibility of going back to the "normalcy" of the 1920s.

Our people are really writing a new song and the phrase "winning the peace" means some very concrete things to them. I think it is beginning to mean Mr. Wallace's "pint of milk a day" guaranteed . . . Mr. Perkins' the people "won't take 'no' for a final answer to their cry for full employment." It means the people can now and I think will now be encouraged to be less scared of the bogey of "the costs" and "the debt." More are saying with Mr. Perkins that "full blast production for a gradually rising standard of living . . . will be physically possible." Many of these leaders tend to find some agreement with him that "this evolutionary progress need not destroy our system of private enterprise . . . Private enterprise will enter upon an era of unparalleled activity." However, they also agree that government must enter fields where private finance cannot enter "without assuming risks that are too great to take with other people's money" . . . that, "to build up a mass consumption great enough to use this mass production," government will also have to make "a bold and daring use of long term credits."

Certainly we can conclude that more of our leaders in government and business than ever before are now beginning to implement battle cries to destroy a slave world, to put a free world in its place. They are on the verge of writing into our state papers a Bill of Economic Rights and Duties to parallel the Civil and Political Bills already included in the Charters.

On my desk stands a bronze statue by Alfeo Faggi. The light of my lamp evokes the muscles of a powerful man. "Depression 1934" Faggi called it . . . himself momentarily cast down by a sick society. "Reservoirs of Power" would be a better name—for, while the total posture is one of being bowed down . . . "depressed" . . . it is not one of being crushed. Every muscle is taut, coiled to spring up—to carry on, to build anew, to create. I saw a fine man beaten down like that once in a dreadful bare hand fist fight. And even as he was forced down on his knees I saw his spirit coil his muscles, pour strength into them from hidden reservoirs of power. And springing up at the tenth count, when all seemed lost, he beat his adversary into submission.

↑ ↑ ↑

As I write our world seems beaten down and the moment is at the tenth count. But our world is like that man; muscles are taut, coiled to spring up, to carry on, to build anew, to create. Our spirit is even now pouring strength into them to win the peace—that is, Tomorrow's war at home which starts up again when the armistices occur in Today's war abroad.

AMERICA DESIGNS FOR
A WORLD OF ORDER

Scholarship, Design, and Practical Life

It has long been a truism of modern history that whatever was honored by a people's students would only much later be cultivated by its politicians and business men. Scholarship on the social scene—practical administration of government, business, and industry—was rarely recognized as an indispensable integral part in the design and operation of the social order. But as the economic system stalled in deeper and broader periods of unemployment . . . as either private or public initiative, working alone, failed again and again to keep the social system running evenly . . . as the necessity for co-operative-total-design was recognized by more students and statesmen—this gap between scholarship and practical life shortened.

From the turn of the century a new attitude slowly emerged. Scientific management in all its ramifications became a vogue. Private as well as public corporations spent hundreds of millions of dollars per year on purely "scientific" as well as technical research. Thus, as the

business men installed men of design at the very forefront of their organizations . . . as government proved
the vast social value of the scientist and the engineer in
the departments and bureaus of Agriculture, Reclamation, Health, Forestry, Commerce, Standards, what not,
the lag of practice behind theory and design shortened.
Finally the two-fold impact of the world's Great Depression and the interregnum of Dictatorship brought
us to the point of actual world revolution and the gap
was obliterated; distinguished scholars were incorporated
quickly into both government and business.

As a result, a thrilling event is taking place before our
eyes and every American must become aware of it. Confronted by the drastic necessity of taking thought on a
vast scale to keep our social system running—of designing our collective life together in order that we may live
our individual ones—a team of confident and creative
men and women is coming together to do it. Here are
engineers, business men, farmers, professional social scientists, social workers, creative artists—nearly every kind
of trained, experienced knowledge needed to make overall designs for a new America in a new world is at hand.
As the world comes to a revolutionary crisis our practical administrators, academic scholars and poets are providing most of the kinds of knowledge and feeling
needed.

Most of the kinds needed—not all. Two are missing—
labor and education.

But again I say: Now is the moment . . . America is
the place . . . the forces are assembling . . . the energies are being mustered.

A Key Group Begins to Create New Designs for American Life

One fact has become crystal clear as a result of the changes of a quarter century—we must design our lives. Drift and muddle will no longer serve us. Even the man on the street has lost patience with that. Our leaders recognize that now they must sit down together and design. They even suggest that by taking thought we *can* actually add a cubit to our stature!

I use the term "design" rather than "plan" to convey the idea of professional competence, of rigorous documentation, of organized knowledge, of responsible care, that we are called upon to employ at this moment. It has been an indispensable part of western man's creative vocabulary throughout his entire history. Neither the engineer nor the artist can work apart from it—each must design before he builds. In the same way the social engineers now coming to life to reconstruct modern society must design with infinite care, resting their structure on the most profound concepts and tested practices of man's history.

This requires above all a central Council of Design to envisage and direct the whole enterprise. And the exciting fact, as stated in Chapter I, is that for some years the personnel of the needed leadership has been assembling at Washington; already it approximates a kind of "Key Group." At its very center are members of the President's original advisers—Henry Wallace and Harry Hopkins, such groups as the National Resources Planning Board, and other leaders from business and engineering and the social sciences brought together by them. Here is a new non-punitive "Brain Trust"—less feared and less scoffed at by business and industrial leaders because part of its very nucleus is drawn from their own ranks.

Mr. Wallace, leader of the key group, embraces much of the experience needed to create designs for an abundant America. He is author of the most discussed idealistic interpretation of America in our times—"The Price of a Free World Victory" . . . Chairman of the powerful Economic Defense Board, now as Vice-President given the task of weaving the production boom of the war into a post-war peace economy. Near him as Executive Director of the Bureau of Economic Warfare is Milo Perkins, a successful Texas manufacturer who retired young to join Wallace in working out the practical design and operation of governmental enterprise. Standing beside the idealist-farmer and business-man-practitioner in government is Harry Hopkins, professionally trained and experienced social worker; since 1933 the President's closest and most trusted single adviser in the Two Wars. Also, an important group of successful business men has now joined the government in the fighting of the Two Wars. To name only five: William M. Batt . . . John D. Biggers . . . W. Averill Harriman . . . Donald M. Nelson . . . Marriner S. Eccles.

Associated with these and other practical men of business, agriculture, and social work are two scores of professional social scientists who have come out of the universities and research institutions of the country to join the march of science-in-government. An important facet of this potential "Council of Design for America" is the National Resources Planning Board and its predecessors:

The National Planning Board and the Committee on National Land Problems, the National Resources Board and the National Resources Committee. Since the beginning of the New Deal government this central design group has been making and publishing positive studies of our natural and human resources. Some of these bid fair to be long remembered in the annals of welfare-social-engineering government. In the Appendix, "What to Read," I refer to several conspicuous ones. Under the general supervision of Secretaries Ickes, Wallace, Perkins, Dern, and Roper, this Board has had the staff services of such distinguished social engineers as: Charles W. Eliot, Morris L. Cooke, Harlow S. Persons, M. L. Wilson . . . such social scientists as Charles E. Merriam, William F. Ogburn, Wesley Mitchell, Charles H. Judd, Warren S. Thompson, Frank Lorimer, E. B. Wilson, Carter Goodrich.

In other departments, bureaus, and boards are such distinguished professional social scientists as:

—Adolph A. Berle, Jr.: former lawyer and Professor of Law at Columbia University . . . Under-Secretary of State . . . author, with Gardiner C. Means, of *The Modern Corporation* . . . designer of a new credit plan known as "Capital Credit Banks."
—Gardiner C. Means: former Columbia Professor of Economics . . . one of the chief coordinating officers working with the trained economists now active in a dozen Executive branches at Washington.
—Mordecai Ezekiel: author of *$2500 A Year* . . . deviser of a plan of "Jobs for all through industrial expansion."
—Alvin H. Hansen: Harvard Professor of Economics . . . consultant of the Federal Reserve Board and the National Resources Planning Board . . . author of the widely dis-

cussed pamphlet of the latter Board—*After the War—Full Employment.*

Rounding out this group are leaders of practical experience in professional government research. At their head is Harold D. Smith: Director of the Federal Budget, really the President's "Business Manager" . . . successful practical director of administrative research in Detroit and Kansas.

Such a government personnel is varied indeed, but the list thus far ignores one of the great areas that has been recognized by Mr. Roosevelt and Mr. Hopkins—namely the arts. The contribution of the New Deal Government made through the creation of the various Federal Arts Projects will live long in history. Witness:

—the Federal Writers Project, which, under the design direction of Henry Alsberg and John D. Newsom, has written and published fifty-one "Guides" to the various states and possessions.

—the creation and operation for five years of the Federal Theatre Project . . . bravely and competently described by its artist-director Hallie Flanagan in her book *Arena*, after an ignorant and insensitive Congress had killed it.

—the Index of American Design inspired by a brave, modest, and imaginative American artist—Ruth Reeves.

—the Federal Art Project led by Holger Cahill and the corresponding enterprise of the Treasury led by Edward Bruce.

—the Federal Music Project, developing into scores of community bands and symphony orchestras and other musical contributions . . . bringing into the service of music in government such artists as Charles Seeger and his wife, Katherine Crawford.

Meanwhile, what of education? To deal with "the

Youth Problem" (studied systematically and effectively since 1935 by the American Youth Commission of the Rockefeller financed American Council on Education), the New Deal created two new agencies—the Civilian Conservation Corps and the National Youth Administration. Government research and design have received a contribution from the field of education through such leaders as Charles H. Judd on the staff of the National Resources Committee, later the National Resources Planning Board . . . Floyd Reeves on the staff of the TVA and other groups . . . William F. Russell as Director of the Alien Education project, and many others. However, as far as the building of a new national spirit to carry through the reconstruction after the war is concerned, little or nothing has been done. But more about that great need later.

And what about the Congress? Will it coöperate with Messrs. Roosevelt, Wallace, *et al.* in the creating of designs for a new and better America? Suppose the Executive can make the plan; will the Congress let it be carried out? Were this essay an attempt to review such questions systematically I could make both a good case and a bad one for Congress. I could show that it had revealed its utter incompetence in leadership on matters of taxation, inflation, price control, labor, such trivia as "pensions and gasoline for Congressmen," of isolationism and downright interference with the war effort, and of demagoguery of the worst kind.

On the other hand, I could point out that the 77th Congress, compared to past War Congresses, was, as one commentator said, "almost a model of speedy and effective action": witness—its declaration of war, the passage of bills giving the President needed powers, the authorization of unprecedented drafts of man power, appropriation bills doubling the legal limit of the national debt, its leadership in expanding the Army and the Navy, its exposure of graft and inefficiency through the Truman and other Committees. Especially would I deal in great detail with the spectacular work of Senator Joseph C. O'Mahoney of Wyoming and his Temporary National Economic Committee, whose reports now total 20,000 printed pages and whose findings are based on the researches and testimony of several hundred experts over a period of three years. Here in TNEC's library is nothing less than a stirring message to the American people that they can now have the abundant life and a challenge to them to take the necessary steps to get it. Certainly here, from the Congress itself, is wonderful material for a Design for America.

✓ ✓ ✓

This galaxy of skilled, top-ranking designers and executives actively at work in government is indeed a new and exciting phenomenon. Since 1933 they have come from every phase of the culture but two: from professional government and government research . . . mechanical engineering . . . business leadership . . . farm leadership . . . social welfare—including public health, diet, and nutrition . . . the creative arts, including graphic and plastic arts, theatre, dance and music, architecture, industrial design. From every phase of the culture but labor and education.

Here is the thing we have dreamed about and pled for and worked for—science in government, research in government, brains in government. Here are the makings of a government of welfare and creative ability . . . a government motivated by good will and guided by brains . . . emerging at the very moment we need it most.

I. Designs for a World of Order

The nature of the two-fold problem which we will confront at the coming of the first armistice is agreed upon by all the students, whether they are of Center-to-Right or Center-to-Left: the first is the certainty of social chaos in each of the destroyed countries and the second is the danger that the domestic economies of all industrial nations will stall, if not break down. Assuming that only the United States, with the collaboration of Great Britain and Russia and our other allies, will be strong enough to meet the gigantic task of serving whole distressed continents, our creative leaders are putting their imaginations and historical resources at the task of preparing plans in advance. They all insist that there must not be any single *world* peace conference—at least not for a long, long time; instead there must be an interim transition period. This will be a period of planned mass hospitalization on a world-wide scale, in which the immediate physical needs of the distressed peoples are taken care of. For this purpose the governments of the United Nations must collaborate in having ships, cargoes, vast stores of foods, medical supplies, clothing, raw materials for housing and industry, transport and communication, and the necessary expert and political personnel ready to rush to countless dying communities.

To the governments and peoples of the democracies the planners—both public and private—say bluntly: avoid the mistakes of 1918-1919. When firing ceases, don't blow the whistle on the factories and call a peace conference. Don't declare an "Armistice" on anything but mass killing and armaments. Don't let the business enterprisers shift for themselves to try to get back to "normalcy" as best they can.

At least a blue print for world order under humane and democratic leadership must be designed now—or else! "Or else" means to let whole sectors of world populations starve, degenerate, become diseased, destroy one another, breed future mass hatreds. We hear hints of such possibilities from our refugee friends—even from sensitive cultivated persons, harassed by memories of Nazi destruction and torture—that nothing will satisfy them but the extermination of the *incipient* Nazism in the entire Germanic culture. A Norwegian and a Pole tell us the geographic limits of their proposed vengeance: "Not till we reach the Rhine," mutters the Pole . . . "Not till we've swept Europe clean as far as the Alps," says the Norse. And as for 400,000,000 righteously indignant Chinese armed and winged to cross the Yellow Sea! Let us be forewarned indeed! Let America and her Allies speak with temporary government, exercising kindly but firm police power—with food, medication, swift education—in time! Now, while there is time, let us speak to our own people with a giant program of education for tolerance and sympathy for the throttled peoples of Naziland and Fascistland to dissipate the climate of hate that has already been cultivated.

Thus while we fight Today's War Abroad we must prepare for the Peace and for Tomorrow's War at Home. We must gather and study all the facts and formulate concrete proposals. These staggering problems must be visualized and discussed long in advance of the time when they will have to be solved. If Americans are to lead in world reconstruction we must find agreements among ourselves as to what we are prepared to do. Our worst offense against the world would be to win the war without, as the *Time-Life-Fortune* Editors say: "having arrived at a common conviction among ourselves as to a program to which we would be willing to dedicate the power and influence of our nation." Because of the vast lack of popular understanding of the problems ahead and because of the propagandistic dangers involved, both public and private scholarship-led agencies should do everything in their power not only to report the facts of the situation but interpret them from their respective points of view.

This is what is happening. The scholars, both of the Center-to-Right and the Center-to-Left, agree that

> There are two wars, two fascisms
> . . . and the two are one,
> Tomorrow's war at home
> as well as today's war abroad.

They agree that the Americans' willingness to produce without regard to cost and to give away to the harassed peoples in order to rehabilitate the world will determine not only our world leadership but also our domestic security in the future. We must produce and give away huge quantities of food, clothing, and materials in order to taper off our own war production.

THE PRINCIPAL DILEMMAS

To remind us of the complexities of the post-war

world reconstruction problems that will confront us, I list nine major dilemmas:

1. The question of time: Begin to plan now vs. win the war first and plan afterward . . . Shall we assume a long armistice or a short armistice?

2. Which comes first: Economic reconstruction . . . or . . . World political structure?

3. Begin with the World as in a Revised-League-of-Nations approach vs. begin with "Regions" . . . "Big initiating states" . . . British-American leadership . . . or, United Nations initiative.

4. The dilemma of collective security for the world and military safety of individual nations; otherwise stated: How guarantee the small nations protection against the coalition and one another?

5. The real causes of war: Economic causes ("Have-nots" vs. "Haves", etc.) vs. psychological causes, as held by those who foresee a greedy, aggrandizing war party—in the future and forever more as well as in the past and in the present.

6. The dilemma over the conditions of peace to be imposed upon the defeated nations: are they to be "just" . . . or . . . "vindictive"?

7. The dilemma of Democracy: How "educate" the nations, peoples, war-party-educated, youth now indoctrinated with Fascist philosophy? Shall we send "educators" from democratic nations . . . or . . . rely upon potential democratic nuclei within the Fascist nations? About this "ultimate," however, the United Nations are adamant: on no other criterion or way of life than the "democratic" will they rebuild the world.

8. How to create a strong world order and yet not destroy sovereignty of nations (Regional Federations of limited powers integrated into a World Federation).

9. How to liberate and raise standards of living of "backward" peoples without lowering standards of "advanced" ones?

TEN IMPERATIVES FOR A WORLD
ORGANIZATION FOR DURABLE PEACE

It must provide.

1. The political structure of world and regional organization . . . Constitution and other legal foundations, assemblies, councils, civil service (secretariat), and the like.
2. International security (political and military) . . . disarm the entire world, down to a Police Force to guarantee security for Big Nations as well as Small Nations on some kind of "quota principle."
3. An international economy operated by several-fold participation—representatives of managers, labor, and governments . . . including a central International Labor Office . . . guaranteeing the free flow of credit and trade and a stable world money system . . . the approach to an eventual economy of abundance around the world.
4. International citizenship (psychological)—building a participating sense of "world" citizenship in each "national" citizen.
5. International justice organization . . . World and Regional courts, etc.
6. International coöperation in development of social welfare . . . child and youth welfare . . . health and narcotics control . . . human migration . . . protection and development of "backward" peoples.
7. International Communication System, including postal, telegraph, telephone, wireless . . . Sealed Roads for all enclosed nations, and the like.
8. International organization for intellectual coöperation.
9. International "mandates" over all previously dependent territories and peoples . . . "pooled colonies" and the like.
10. International supervision (interim) of defeated countries and peoples.

BLUE PRINTS FOR WORLD RECONSTRUCTION

As I write, six plans in the fairly definite "blue print" stage have been published and various other systematic statements of principles have been made. These proposals for world organization can be stated briefly as nine alternatives:

1. The Western Hemisphere plan. (George Jaffin in *New World Constitutional Harmony: A Pan-Americanadian Panorama* discusses Hemispheric Union based on ideological commonality.)
2. Anglo-Saxon (Britain and America) leadership (Clarence Streit: *Union Now* and *Union Now with Britain* and *Fortune* Editors: The United States in a New World: I. Relations with Britain, May 1942 . . . II. Pacific Relations, August 1942.) . . . policing . . . protection and development of the world. In the case of the *Fortune* Editors this is perilously close to Anglo-Saxon imperialism, with national normalcy—*laissez faire*-private-enterprise—as the technique.
3. Regional Plans. (Such as outlined by George Soule and *The New Republic* Editors in "The Lessons of Last Time," *The New Republic*, February 2, 1942.)
4. The United Nations approach. (Such as the World Citizens Association reports: *The United Nations, What They Are, What They May Become* and *The United Nations on the Way* in which Henri Bonnet discusses the organization of a United Nations Political Council.)
5. World Federation Plans, including Regional Federations.
    a. Economic plans: Hans Heymann: *Plans for Permanent Peace* and *Justice for All* (proposal for a Bank of Nations) and Otto Tod Mallery: *Economic Order and Durable Peace*.
    b. Complete World Federation structure . . . guaranteeing disarmament, providing for economic

structures and operation: Ely Culbertson: *The World Federation Plan.*

6. League of Nations Plan . . . revival of and modification in the light of history.

    a. Commission for the Study of Organization of Peace: two preliminary reports in *International Conciliation* (April 1941 and April 1942) . . . tentative blue prints in preparation.

    b. Institute on World Organization, Washington, D. C. This group is largely composed of members of the former Secretariat of the League of Nations. (See their Symposium on *World Organization*, published under the auspices of the American Council on Public Affairs.)

7. The Good Neighbor plans, depending heavily on the "Good Neighbor" policy of the United States and Latin America, sometimes called the Good Will plans in which the victor is willing to make economic sacrifices in order to construct a durable peace. (See Lionel Curtis: *World Order* . . . Glenn Clark: *Two or Three Gathered Together* . . . Roswell Barnes: *A Christian Imperative, Our Contribution to World Order* . . . Louis Adamic: *Two-Way Passage* . . . Hoover and Gibson: *Problems of Lasting Peace*).

Opposed to the Foregoing—

8. Geopolitics: Rule by the victors . . . in the case of the United Nations this is supposed to mean a "democratic" kind of nationalism and "benevolent imperialism" . . . in the case of the Fascist-Dictatorship nations it means ruthless "Geopolitics"—domination of the earth by The Master Race, governed by The Master Class. For the Germanic brand see Karl Haushofer: *Power and Earth* . . . for the Anglo-Saxon, Nicholas John Spykman: *America's Strategy in World Politics.* Robert Strausz-Hupé: *Geopolitics* gives the clearest and most incisive interpretation of the whole problem and trend.

9. The Extreme Isolationists . . . "America First" . . . "no entangling alliances" . . . let Europe "stew in her own juice."

THE PROPOSED PLANS

CULBERTSON'S WORLD FEDERATION PLAN

Ely Culbertson's brilliant and practical plan is organized around a permanent world government composed of a World President, 11 World Trustees, 11 World Supreme Court Judges, 11 World Court of Equity Judges, and 55 World Senators (five Senators are to be chosen from each Regional Federation to represent these groups: Agriculture, Education, Science, Capital, Labor).

The World Federation may be likened to a world-wide trust. There is a Holding Company (the World Federation) partially controlling eleven Regional "Subsidiaries"; each Regional Subsidiary, in turn, partially controls a number of State Subsidiaries (sovereign states) which are the operating units. The whole is regulated by a Social Contract, based on the freedom of sovereign states, wherein the duties and responsibilities of the Holding Company and all its subsidiaries are mutually limited. Back of the Social Contract, there is the Court. Back of this Court, there is a police force—the World Police. And in the World Police is a psychological mechanism which actually holds the whole system together —the Quota Force Principle.

This plan has been designed to "provide for both the collective security of the world and the military safety of individual nations. It proposes "a new method of armament, composition and distribution of the national armed forces of each state, by means of which the government of the World Federation obtains an overwhelming police force of its own based on the monopoly of heavy weapons without jeopardizing the capacity of individual states to resist any aggression." The armed forces will be composed of a quota of officers and men recruited from the citizens of each "initiating state," called the National Contingent, and a collective quota— the Mobile Corps—units of the same nationality recruited from member states other than the initiating states which form part of the sovereign federation. The quota table gives the following distribution of the National Contingents and their armament:

	Initiating State	*Regional Federation*
20%	United States	—American
15%	Britain & the Dominions	—British
15%	Russia	—Russian
4%	France	—Latin
4%	Germany	—Germanic
4%	Poland	—Middle European
4%	China	—Chinese
4%	Turkey	—Middle Eastern
4%	India	—Indian
2%	Malaysian Federation	—Malaysian
2%	Japan	—Japanese
22%	Mobile Corps of the non-initiating states	

Fortune EDITOR'S PLAN:
BRITISH-AMERICAN CONTROL

The point of view of the scholarship of the Center-to-Right is illustrated by the reports of the Editors of *Time,* *Life,* and *Fortune.* Assuming that "the United States

is likely to emerge from a United Nations victory
as the most powerful nation in the world" and that it is
the desire of a large part of the American public to
realize Tennyson's dream of "The Parliament of Man,
the Federation of the World," Dr. Raymond Leslie Buell
and his staff of specialists sketch a post-war program in
the first of "a series of reports on potential courses for
democratic action" entitled "The United States in a
New World." The nub of this proposal is that "the
United States can and should work out with Britain and
the Dominions a program of leadership. This program
should outmode past imperialism but at the same time it
must work toward a world unity." Russia and China are
not specifically included in the statement, but references
to the United Nations are made.

According to the Buell plan the Axis powers are to be
disarmed and surrendered to committees of the United
Commands. They will be policed by such Commands in
accordance with the Atlantic Charter during the Reconstruction Period—which may last several years—maintaining law and order and carrying out the decisions of
the United Nations. This may lead to "creating the basis
for a permanent International Legion which could eventually be used by a new World Association for police
purposes in any part of the world." It is proposed "to
work out a system of international security, to take effect
at the end of the Reconstruction Period, making possible
a general reduction of armaments. Within this system
regional arrangements such as the creation of a European
federal militia would find their place."

The Luce organization commits America to world
participation and coöperation from now on, and no with-

drawing. World economic life should be guided by "a common economic policy—the creation of a free market area," and America and Great Britain "should conclude at once a series of agreements aimed at creating a single free area for enterprise, making possible new opportunities after this war for exports and imports and bringing about rising national income." This will "implement the Atlantic Charter and be a step toward creating liberal trading areas applying eventually to all the United Nations . . . The United States and the United Kingdom should abolish all tariff restrictions on their own trade." The editors urge that the United States and Britain "assume a common responsibility" for demobilization, but the programs adopted during this Reconstruction Period should aim to expand fields for private endeavor rather than to contract them.

The free market plan is also advocated as a measure for relieving distress. "The problem of poverty can be solved only by an increase in wealth and an expanding economy" . . . "81 per cent of the world's population ekes out an existence on considerably less than $10 a week per bread winner." Therefore, the United States must be prepared to make enormous outright grants of money for the rebuilding of the destroyed nations. It "should create a Reconstruction Fund of several billion dollars taken from its huge gold reserves. Nations lacking working capital in the reconstruction period should draw against this fund in accordance with a plan approved by the United Nations." (This Reconstruction Fund would not exclude a national plan temporarily allocating food and shipping, raw materials in the Reconstruction Period.) This is "to the interests of the United States,

the world's wealthiest power, to prevent the return of
. . . international anarchy." The Editors say that "such
a Fund together with the $7,000,000,000 of frozen assets
in the United States should give impoverished nations
the working capital necessary to participate in the free
market area without burdening them with a new debt,
and thus avoid the catastrophic mistakes bound up with
the reparations and inter-Allied debts after World War
I."

The Editors themselves are uncertain as to the practica-
bility of this proposal for an "Americo-British free
market area." They say that it will probably seem "chaotic and futile. The bureaucratic planning school [ap-
parently they mean the various Center-to-Left groups]
will condemn the idea on the ground that the market
will not 'work'; others will oppose it on the ground that
vested interest in heavily protected industry, labor, and
agriculture will be too strong to allow its adoption."
There is disagreement and some misgiving among the
scholars and publicists of the Center-to-Left as to the
real intent and probable effect of this program.

Some link this report with Mr. Luce's two annual edi-
torials on *The American Century*[1] and interpret it, as did
Miss Freda Kirchwey, Editor of *The Nation*, in an editorial on February 28, 1942, as Anglo-American imperialism in the international field, and as back-to-free-
enterprise on the domestic front. There are indeed un-
explained enigmas in the proposal. While it advocates
the setting up of a world police force, free trade the
world over, and American humanitarian initiative and
financial support of the reconstruction of the distressed

[1] *Life*, February 17, 1941, and February 16, 1942.

nations, it is not at all clear how far the proposal would militate against the interjection of social capital into the production systems of each of the individual nations.

At any rate, it is a vigorous forthright example of America studying and speaking. Whether the *Time-Life-Fortune* group moves Right or Left they have, as they said, moved away from "the hesitant thinking of the thirties."

The Center-to-Left, represented by such students as Mr. Soule, proposes the gradual creation of a kind of regional-world federalism, something on the order of TVA regionalism under the United States government. Under this plan the first task is to group many localities together according to their regions and then to create diffused sovereignty among many international economic and cultural units such as the British Commonwealth of Nations, the Soviet Union, North and South America, a federated Europe composed of sub-regions—Scandinavia, the central and western countries, the Mediterranean countries. The government is to be self-created over each region, each locality relinquishing the barest minimum of economic-political sovereignties to the regional government and the regional units in turn giving up as few as possible to the world federation; the latter being especially in control of world police, armaments, natural resources, and economic sanctions.

Streit: *Union Now*

Clarence Streit's proposal is a union of English-speaking democracies, with a constitution modeled on the American system of federal union. The citizens of member countries will also be world citizens with an equal voice in the representative Union government. The functions of the Union government will be to make war and peace for all its members . . . govern their foreign relations and their non-self-governing territory . . . provide a common defense force, a common free trade market, currency, postal and communication systems. The freedoms of speech, press, religion, and peaceful association are to be guaranteed . . . and each member democracy retains the right of individual national government and all rights not specifically granted to the Union government. The plan also provides for the admission of new nations and colonies on an equal basis with the founders—so that eventually the Union will be the government of all mankind and armament will be reduced to a world police force.

Two Plans for Economic Reconstruction

Opposed to the "political-reconstruction-planners" are those who would build economic remedies first. They assume that if the armistice is long enough "a post-war program of gigantic global expenditures administered by United Nations commissions will raise the economic standards of all nations so high that there will no longer be a reason for wars. Associated with them are all of the "economy of abundance" people and the peace foundation people who believe with Culbertson "in the necessity of a *long term* program of economic reconstruction in order to repair the shattered foundations of the world." And they insist further: "We must never again neglect economics in making a future peace."

I. *The Heymann banking and credit plan* for international economic organization is conceived in terms of a three-fold world plan: 1. the social sphere—embodied in a reformed International Labor Office; 2. the political sphere—called a Federal World Authority; and 3. the economic sphere, functioning through a Bank of Nations. The Bank of Nations is given the task of unifying and coördinating the world community through three branch banks: the Western Hemisphere Bank, the European Bank, and the Oriental Bank and their affiliates in each country. Specifically, the Bank of Nations is to be given the power to issue currency and create credit, and to deal with such special problems as international labor migration, unemployment insurance, crop insurance, raw materials, gold.

Dr. Heymann thinks of this plan as "Social Capitalism"—a merging of the ideas of the classical social philosophers and the economic basis for the democratic world of tomorrow. He presented an early edition of this plan in 1922 when Walter Rathenau asked him to prepare a memorandum for the Conference of Genoa. At that time, however, it was considered "premature."

II. *The Mallery Economic Union Plan* is built up step by step on the "enlightened self-interest of the moment" rather than imposed as a ready-made overall organization. A complete world Economic Union can only be built up gradually, but it is important that we begin now. His immediate proposal is that the United States take the initiative by choosing partners and forming the nucleus of a post-war Economic Union *now*. Such a Union would be modeled on the Governing Body of the

International Labor Organization with a three-fold Board of Managers representing organized workers, organized managers, and governments. On the foundation of the Hull Reciprocal Trade Agreement Program an Inter-American Bank could be organized now as a preliminary to setting up the Economic Union later. Eventually, the world Economic Union's main functions would be to draw up Promotional Trade Agreements between states to replace the Restraint of Trade Agreements that helped to bring on the war . . . to establish a Commission for Territorial Administration which will draw up a plan for the provision of equal access to raw materials and markets . . . to enforce international fair trade practices . . . to regulate international cartels . . . to organize joint international action against depressions.

Mr. Mallery takes what he calls a "pragmatic, realistic view" because he prefers "economic bargains likely to be kept" to "political agreements likely to be broken."

II. On the Domestic Front: Transition from Armed Warfare to Peace

I have dealt with America's role in world rehabilitation because of its inextricable interdependence with the task of avoiding the collapse of our domestic economic system when the deficit-financed, full-employment war-boom is over. It is becoming increasingly clear to students of the problem that only through all-out participation in world rehabilitation can we possibly make the transition to peace-time activities without a renewal of the Great Depression. I repeat what was said at the beginning of this essay: only by producing full tilt and giving away billions to raise standards of living all over the world can we put enough purchasing power into the hands of our own people to keep our system running.

And that is the problem to be solved by vigorous leadership of our gathering "Council of Design" in Washington. First, the position of the National Resources Planning Board and its distinguished consultant Dr. Alvin Hansen.

MEMORANDA OF PLANS-IN-PROGRESS FROM THE NRPB

In two important publications[2] the Board has brought the problem to the country's attention. It warns against the danger that the switch-back of not less than 26,000,-000 workers from war to peace activities may come about only by the stoppage of plants, the unemployment of more millions of workers than ever before in our history (the number 20,000,000 is being more than whispered in Washington), and a decrease in income from 120 to 80 or even 70 billion dollars.

The Board gives the American people clear objectives for their coming effort: (1) to maintain full employment at an annual national income of not less than $100,-000,000,000 (1940 dollars) . . . (2) to retain a 40-hour working week and 50-week year at high wages without using the youth or the aged . . . (3) to decentralize post-war emergency activities as far as possible, using to the utmost our system of modified free enterprise . . . (4) to enable every human being within our boundaries to realize progressively the promise of American life in food, shelter, clothing, medical care, education, work, rest, home life, opportunity to advance, adventure, and

[2] NRPB: *After Defense—What?* (1941) and Hansen: *After the War —Full Employment* (1942; approved and distributed by the Board).

the basic freedoms . . . (5) to make Up-Building America the key-note of the post-war program, including construction activities which will add to the National Estate and service activities which will end malnutrition and increase the vitality, health, skill, productivity, knowledge, and happiness of the American people, and thus add to our wealth and well-being.

To realize these aims this section of the federal government's key group proposes a positive program which can be put into effect right now. Plans for demobilization, a program for public works, government coöperation with industry and plans for the training of professional workers are already under way. New forms of social security and programs for relief and work relief must be put into operation. The government, say Dr. Hansen and the NRPB, must undertake the responsibility of leading in the rebuilding of America with a program of

urban redevelopment projects, rural rehabilitation, low-cost housing, express highways, terminal facilities, electrification, flood control, reforestation . . . a public health program . . . higher educational standards . . . an enrichment of the spiritual and material resources of our American way of life.

These Hansen and NRPB bulletins constitute a kind of preliminary Memorandum of Plans-in-Progress from one section of our central Council of Design, designed to stimulate wide-spread public study and discussion and so to help build public opinion.

✦ ✦ ✦

Meanwhile other officers of the key group are putting

out their own Memoranda. They all ask: What steps can be taken now, while the war is on, to make private enterprise work in the transition to peace? Or rather, in the spirit of the American Way of employing both private and public facilities: What can government and various private enterprises do? Anxious to avoid government intervention or ownership and operation, they are trying to envisage all possible steps to employ private initiative to the full. I comment briefly on proposals to deal with four phases of the problem.

1. Full Employment through Free Flow of Credit

The students in the key group—business men as well as scholars—insist that the central obstruction to the smooth functioning of the whole economy is the finance-credit structure. All agree that for a half century American industry—indeed all economic expansion—has been financed, hence controlled, by "bankers" and recognize the need for shifting that control to the producers themselves.

A. A. Berle, Jr., testifying before TNEC, described the process from which business men are trying their best to escape as "the bottle neck of finance capitalism," insisting that "most business men who are not in banking" want a "radical over-hauling of the banking system." Mr. Berle proposed the formation of a new system of Capital Credit Banks to give long-term credits which experience has proved the commercial banks are loath to give. These banks can be either government-owned or private; the former, if private initiative did not create them promptly and operate them successfully. This proposal would shift control, essentially replacing the present investment function of Wall Street, but the new banks "would be more responsible to the public and carried on by groups which by their nature assume greater responsibility for maintaining a continuing economic flow."

While not agreeing with the government ownership possibilities of what some people are calling "Berle's Banks," students tend to support the trend now under way "from banker-guidance to producer-guidance."

Mr. Milo Perkins, another of the key group, suggests that if private investment banking does not soon provide a mechanism by which credit can be obtained by any worthy prospective employer, government may have to use part of its twenty billion gold reserves for the stock of "government credit banks." Here is a hint of a new set of Government Yardstick Corporations paralleling TVA and others. A glimpse of the potentialities of this process is given by Mr. Perkins:

If banks financed inexpensive homes at cost, with extremely low interest, monthly payments for houses would go down by nearly a third. If they financed municipal improvements in the same manner, the costs to local taxpayers for roads and sewer systems and hospitals would be cut down by nearly one-half.

Thus a construction boom would be stimulated without using Federal appropriated money.

It's worth noting that even a daring over-haul of the long-term debt side of fiscal capitalism would not hurt industrial capitalism and might even help it.

Concerning the hundreds of millions of idle savings

pouring each month into such enterprises as the great insurance companies, the new social designers ask: What can government do to persuade or to force these savings to flow into productive enterprise? One step, learned from the experience of FHA insurance of home mortgages, is to guarantee the security of its use.

Thus, although blue prints and threats are not yet in evidence, the key group in government is beginning to make two things fairly clear: First—that the bottle neck of finance-capitalism must be broken with real efficiency and despatch, preferably by private banking. Second—that government's chief role should not be to own credit institutions or to interject social capital—but to compel private investment and to guarantee security to the investor. In all of the testimony and pronouncements there· is a warning note: Let private finance-capitalism put its house in smoothly functioning order—or else!—government will move in and take over.

2. *Full Employment through Designed Taxation.*

As we have seen in Chapter III, throughout the First Industrial Revolution most economic concepts were defined negatively. Taxation was no exception—in spite of a half century of free lance suggestions (Henry George *et al.*) for using it positively to maintain an efficiently functioning economy. And until recently our Executive leadership and Congress have tended to build a tax plan which would drive money away from investment, rather than develop positive taxation to force savings into enterprises which will employ more people.

But under the continuing stale-mate of the Great Depression the search for positive governmental action to

help make private enterprise work—at full employment
—led to an increasing discussion of various types of "incentive taxation." One group in Congress—the Senate
Finance sub-committee—recently advocated such an experiment in which tax-exempt funds must "be used in
the direct employment of labor and materials." Other
members of the key group are also preaching positive
taxation: "Tax idle money into use." "Employ the tax
system to stimulate rather than to stifle investment." Exempt from the tax all income which is used to put people
to work. L. H. Parker, experienced tax schedule maker
for the Joint Congressional Committee on Taxation,
offered a three-fold plan: Impose a normal tax, a surtax,
and in addition a "super tax" from which any business
man would be exempt by meeting "incentive" needs of
investment. Others have proposed "merit-rating" schemes
by which business taxes vary with amounts of employment provided.

In the American Way of letting proposals come from
any part of the citizenry and having government listen
as well as make its own original suggestions, the Senate
Finance sub-committee recently held hearings and
summed up the combined judgments thus:

The pace with which money flows to our plant and equipment replacements and to expansions, determines whether
times are good or bad . . . The savings to compensatory
tax exemptions would be used to put men to work directly
by business, instead of being paid by government and dis-
bursed on public works.

Their report was made in 1939 and neither the Executive
nor the Congress has acted on it. But it does indicate

the nature of the trend of thinking and holds promise of action when the need is urgent at the close of armed warfare.

3. *Wages and Profits, Full Employment and Prices*

Recurring through the public discussion of the problem of designing the economy is the question: What should government do about prices, wages, profits—and monopoly? The answer of government officials in pre-depression, pre-war years was—"as little as possible" . . . "the less government the better" . . . "Let economic principles settle such questions." But too often the result was control concentrated in monopoly enterprises with enormous profits and high prices, frequently "fixed" . . . and many small enterprises killed off or stifled. The attitude of the gathering Design Group, therefore, is very different. It is one of positive interest, rather than one of aloofness and indifference.

On the basis of its 1940 report which showed that in "prosperous" periods profits always outran wages, and were not accompanied by reductions in prices, the NRPB said emphatically: "It is essential that the buying power of consumers (including payments to wage earners and raw material producers, such as farmers and miners) increase more rapidly than profits and dividend payments." Moreover as shown in testimony before TNEC, increased wages do not mean reduced profits—in the long run. For example, to produce a ton of steel costs $65.90 with the plant at full capacity—and $99.40 when the plant is running at 20 per cent capacity.

So the Design Group tends to ask: What can government do after the war to help enterprise operate a busy low-priced economy, rather than an idling high-priced one? How to encourage small enterprise? And its tentative answers are: go into the whole matter of costs, prices, and profits . . . break down monopoly enterprises . . . proceed vigorously against racketeers in labor as well as in business. Thurman Arnold's activities against violators of the anti-trust laws is evidence that the key group is not withholding action until the post-war period.

4. *Why Is Labor Not in the Design Group?*

As the personnel of the Design Group that must compass new master plans for a new America assembles, labor is missing. This group is much more completely organized than ever before and, thanks to the Wagner Act, now holds a bargaining position on a par with capital. Yet positive leadership in social design does not emerge.

Perhaps, you say, the cause lies in its history. Like every other phase of economic life during the First Industrial Revolution labor's philosophy and program was essentially negative. For a hundred years it was an all-out offense-defense army fighting the battle of hours, wages, conditions, and collective bargaining. And a good fight it has fought—and won. It may be that the organized workers have felt down-trodden and on the defensive so long that even today the "hate" hang-over stays with them to the exclusion of all else. Moreover, labor is caught—even as monopoly capitalism has been caught—in an interregnum of dirty racketeering. Some of it, as the Department of Justice has recently proved, is actual violation of the law, much of it is sheer power-politics of selfish, aggrandizing bosses. While government is cleaning up some of it and will continue to do so vigorously, labor obviously must put its own house in order.

Labor must now replace its negative leadership with positive leadership, or it will become a merely tolerated nonentity in the new social design. It must discover creative brains among its young personnel and put those brains to work at the Council Table of Design for an abundant America. Labor men are close to the processes of production and distribution, and know those processes internally in their own terms as well as any brigade of management. If labor is to share the redesign, reconstruction, and operation of our giant economic system after the war, if it is to have an active responsible share in management, it must earn it by a revelation of creative ability and a willingness to collaborate in the design for an abundant America.

A Great Collaborative Adventure

This brief summary of some of the basic ideas that emerge from the interviews, testimony, speeches, and writing of the Design Group in Washington gives a hint of the body of important Memoranda of Plans-in-Progress that is being built. We have now in our National Executive courageous imaginative students, experienced in many walks of American life, rigorously analyzing the coming post-war problem and boldly sketching new designs for what they see is a new day.

Their studies of the basic economic problems show advancing agreement on four points: *First*—in the postwar transition the economic system need not collapse, or even stall, the dire warnings of the Hart-Prentis type of freedom-from-restraint free-enterprisers to the contrary notwithstanding. *Second*—the very assumption of our responsibilities in rehabilitating the world will help prevent it by compelling us to continue to operate our domestic economic system at near-peak load; this will contribute to tapering off from war to peace smoothly. *Third*—America need not be stopped from running her economic system by financial fears—inability "to pay," "too big a public debt," and the like. *Fourth*—America, like all the industrialized nations, will never return to the "normalcy" of uncontrolled free enterprise. In short: run the economic system on the same theory in peace-time as in war-time, accept six per cent as a fair profit, and forget the bogey of the public debt.

"But," I hear members of the Center-to-Right opposition say, "isn't this a proposal to 'socialize' the economic system?" The reactionary bloc of the Dies Committee, the Prentis-wing of the NAM and such of its mouthpieces as George Sokolsky, the Chaillaux-Americanism Committee of the American Legion, and Elizabeth Dilling (if she's saying anything these days) will all shout: "This is Communism."

On the contrary, this is "the American Way." Not only is a great society of abundance to be built—but it is to be a coöperative commonwealth. We Americans will not tolerate social changes imposed by authoritarian oppressive measures; our whole tradition will protest the imposition of external control upon our joint and individual enterprises. If social control is to be imposed, we will do it ourselves voluntarily by the free play of discussion and majority vote. This is the American Way—the nearest approach to democracy we know.

Dr. Hansen and the NRPB make the need for collaboration very clear.

The problem we face when the war ends is too big and complicated to be solved by the workers, the farmers, the business men or the Government alone . . . nothing less than energetic and intelligent team work will make it possible for us to move over from defense to peace, while maintaining full employment.

Private industry alone cannot do the job, but active initiation of an all-out production program under the leadership of the government will "vitalize and invigorate private enterprise." The "one center of responsible coördinating power through which we can all act together is the Government," and to build a coöperative program "will require *advance* thinking, discussing, planning, and organizing for action."

Both government and private scholarship insist upon the collaboration of manufacturers, farmers, and coöperatives with the various branches of government. The national government will bring total sovereignty over any inter-state region nation-wide financing and credit power, and can assemble competent creative designers in every aspect of social engineering. But the actual administration of post-war enterprise, while initiated in many instances by national or state government, must have a "grass-roots" operation. Business men—big and little, but especially little—the big ones make their own —must be given "credit" and helped to manufacture and sell. Coöperatives of farmers and workers and homemakers must be given the same opportunities and resources. But wherever private enterprise dare not undertake the risk or is inert in the doing of it, government must step in and create a massive Government Yardstick

Corporation to stimulate and regulate the production and marketing of goods.

But, warn the conservative free-enterprisers, "It will cost too much!" The scholar in government replies:

> The notion that we cannot finance our own production is quite without foundation . . . from $100 billion income we can raise large tax revenues—large enough to service any level debt likely to be reached and to cover all other Government outlays—and still retain for private expenditures more than we had left in former years under a $70 billion income with lower taxes.

Unconvinced, the back-to-normalcy group repeat: "We can't afford it!"

CAN WE AFFORD ABUNDANCE?

But, reiterates the scholar-in-government: *a people can afford whatever it can produce.* Listen again to Dr. Hansen and the NRPB:

> No country need be impoverished if its productive resources (both capital and human) are intact.
>
> We can afford as high a standard of living as we are able to produce.
>
> We have to make up our minds as a nation that we will not permit a post-war depression to overwhelm us.
>
> We have every reason to expect the national income to rise to around $100 billion in terms of 1940 dollars.
>
> We do not want to run the whole show, we do not want a totalitarian state, we want freedom of enterprise . . . for collective bargaining . . . for coöperative action . . . for choice of occupation.[3]

If, as Comte said, "Ideas rule the world or throw it into

[3] Alvin H. Hansen: *After the War—Full Employment* (National Resources Planning Board, Washington, 1942).

chaos"—then here is one idea the Americans should chant in unison. This is a slogan to galvanize our people into creative social action. Probably one of the two crucial ideas of our time (the other one being that we have the physical and spiritual makings of an abundant civilization) it lies at the very nub of the impasse over the running of the economic system. Every proposal to run the system at full employment in peace as in war brings without fail either the angry expletive "Communist" or the terrified protest, "We can't afford it!" But if the combined judgment of the scholars and business men in government is right, "we can afford as high a standard of living as we are able to produce." If the American people can grasp the full import of this idea now, while the war is on, they can, with the coming of the armistices, continue to run their economic system at full employment. Because of the established fact of our potential physical and spiritual abundance, they can build a free world in the fullest sense. And they can bring it to pass within the next generation. This is not the first time that our people have been urged to run their social system at full employment without regard to the cost, but—now is the moment—for now they are actually confronted by the pragmatic likelihood of success.

What Is the "Cost" of a Thing?

From a tremendous library of documentation it is clear that the very lives of modern industrial peoples, including the Americans, depend upon the smooth functioning of a stable money economy, that—a stable medium of exchange and a stable system of prices and wages. Under such an economy the question of "the cost of a

thing" becomes paramount, for every proposal to use
government funds to employ all the people in peace-
time brings the age-old warning: "we can't afford it."

What, then, does a thing cost? I hear the reply: "Tell
me what the dollar is 'worth' and I'll tell you what the
thing costs."

I don't like that answer, for it tells me little. Alvin
Hansen's affirmation, "We can afford as high a standard
of living as we can produce," rings far truer to me. It
takes me back to Henry Thoreau's definition:

> "The cost of a thing is the amount of what I will
> call life which is required to be exchanged for it."

The cost of a thing is the amount of my life I must give
for it. My life as producer—not as exploiter depending
on money to make money. If I produce it actually with
hands or brains I know full well what it costs. If I can't
do that—lacking materials, land, technology, other physical resources, or the necessary skill—I must produce
something else, things or ideas, and exchange them for
the thing. But the life that I put into the production of
something is the real cost of the thing I buy. This is the
only definition of cost that makes sense to me. Hence
when I ask myself: "Can I afford this thing?" my answer is, "Yes, if I can produce it, or something that can
be exchanged for it."

Modern peoples—including the Americans—must
learn to give that answer in peace as well as in war. We
should be able to, because we fight the war with that
very answer. Can we afford 185,000 airplanes? 120,00c
tanks? A million tons of ships a month? Mr. Roosevelt
and Mr. Nelson answer by asking another question: "Can

we produce them? Have we got the resources in land, metals, fuels, fibers, fertilizers, machine technology, research engineers, technicians, skilled workers? The War Production Board gives the answer of our organized nation: Yes! So we produce them—without regard to the cost. We tax, we double the debt limit, we borrow, and —we produce.

"But this is total war; our lives are at stake!" answer those who would return to a normalcy of scarcity and the balanced budget after the immediate danger is past.

Yes, this is one of the wars we fight . . . Today's war abroad. But, I remind you, we fight Two Wars and when the armistices come Tomorrow's war at home, over running the domestic economic system, will begin again. Then our lives—more important, our souls—will be at stake again. 20,000,000 . . . 30,000,000 . . . 40,000,000 lives and souls. Then, with respect to all our worldly and spiritual goods, we shall face the question: "Can we afford it?"

CAN WE AFFORD THE GOOD LIFE?

A third of the nation is ill-housed; we need 10,000,000 good houses, says the President. Can we afford them? For forty years our leaders in social reconstruction have known our need and have built good houses in one experimental enterprise after another. Every attempt failed; the families who had lived there in slums—the families for whom the new houses were built—moved away to new slums. Why? The new houses "cost too much" . . . rentals were too high, the land, finance, and up-keep costs too great.

Can the American people afford good houses? The

answer, learned from running the war production plant, is "Yes—if we can produce them!" And we *can* produce them! The evidence stands before us—

In the pure architecture of our streamlined skyscraper, In the landscape-fitted lines of our new family houses.

We have the makings—materials, engineers, artists, skilled workers, creative designers. When the armistices come let government guarantee credit and cost and let us produce good houses for our 32,000,000 families. Let us produce without regard to the bookkeeping costs . . . with regard to only one measure: How much of our lives are we willing to give to produce them?

Consider the health of our people. Half of the 3000-odd counties of America have no hospitals. In every one of these women die in childbirth each year . . . human beings suffer and die because of lack of hospitalization. Why? The people in those counties haven't the "money." "We can't afford a hospital."

But we can produce good hospitals . . . we can build and equip and staff them. We have good doctors . . . good surgeons . . . good nurses . . . good medical schools. Knowledge and good will are at hand. We, the American people, have in ourselves the spiritual credit as well as the physical makings with which to build hospitals . . . to develop 30,000,000 healthy children . . . to nourish and nurse their families as well. We can afford a healthy America because we can produce it.

Another example—from education, the true impetus, guide, and control of democracy. After a century of building schools, thousands of American communities still lack the capacity to develop a generation of well-informed, thoughtful, sensitive young people, equipped to meet a world at social crisis. Why? "Costs too much. Can't afford good schools."

Can we build good buildings? We can—efficient and beautiful ones. Do we have good teachers and administrators and technicians? Yes, and we know how to find and develop better ones . . . a great race of true artist-teachers and educational leaders is in the making right now on our continent. A race of courageous and sensitive men and women who beg for the opportunity to push this potentially magnificent civilization around into actual efficiency and beauty. And the only "cost" they recognize is "the amount of the lives of our people that must be given to pay for it."

And so, with every department of American life. Can we afford good poems, . . . good novels . . . profound essays? Have we got creative poets, novelists, essayists? The answer to that question is the only true answer to the other one.

We can afford good pictures if our painters can paint them . . . good statues if our sculptors can carve them . . . good songs if our singers can sing them . . . good theatre if we can grow creative playwrights, artist-directors, stage designers, actors, electricians . . . and sensitive audiences.

Good newspapers and magazines and books? Of course, magnificent ones, we know how to write and print and publish.

Illustrations are without limit.

I say our crisis has precipitated a great idea—an idea to galvanize the American people into creative action: *a people can afford whatever it can produce.*

Positive Creative Leadership Through Government

To realize this great idea a new philosophy . . . a new program ·. . . a new strategy . . . and new tactics must be designed and built. Not by a Man-on-horseback —for America rejects the Great Man Theory and the Way of Dictatorship—but by a cross section of the best technical knowledge, vision and sensitivity, courage and practical experience we can assemble in this country. And that is exactly what has been foregathering under the aegis of national government in Washington. A great collaborative adventure in design and reconstruction is under way.

The Structure of Design Leadership

But the structure of this leadership assembling under national government must be truly land-based; to that extent it must be decentralized. Let the new design come out of America's 20,000 communities. Conceived in the broadest sense "government" in America springs from the day by day interplay of the welter of interest groups which makes up the life of every community. Especially is this revealed in the process by which local government goes on—a kind of zig-zag, compromising give-and-take between assertive individuals and groups: political parties . . . economic organizations . . . neighborhood groups . . . good government groups . . . business and service groups . . . religious groups . . . educational groups.

Each one brings its respective pressure to bear on elected representatives—presenting positive plans or negative demands, persuading legislation and executive action through the weight of its voting power. Back of it all is the American idea: We do it together . . . all shall be heard . . . government by the people. In the coming crisis we shall not only preserve but encourage our fundamental American Way, and I foresee a wealth of suggestion emerging from local study and discussion.

But the actual redesign and reconstruction for our complex continental society can be accomplished only by organized leadership. The constituents of that design leadership have been forming throughout the decades of our Great Transition in a great "planning" movement applying science and technology to social engineering. A single measure of its present status is the Twentieth Century Fund's monograph by Dr. George B. Galloway: *Post-War Planning in the United States*, published in the spring of 1942, which reports the actual planning activities of no less than 112 public and private agencies (not including the 48 State Planning Boards), covering 64 fields of planning. As a result of the activity of the past decade, practically every state government now has a "Planning Board," staffed by competent engineers, agriculturists, foresters, professional government workers, research students, and the like. As an example of important "regional" planning by the national government I remind the reader of the achievements of the Tenessee Valley Authority which I described in Chapter II.

Under this new version of the American Way the outlines of a four-fold Structure of Design Leadership begin to appear:

First: Centered at Washington we have in the key group a potential National Council of Design.

Second: Emerging in various centers of the country are Regional Councils of Design.

Third: In the 48 State Planning Boards we already possess the nucleus of the needed State Councils of Design.

Fourth: In thousands of communities of America, under a nation-wide campaign, alert citizens will form Community Councils of Design.

The main outlines of the national structure will develop in the key group at the nation's capital. There the Master Design for an abundant America will gradually develop. There the direction of the national and state legislation and executive action must be centered. And there the criticism and suggestions of thousands of citizens, publicists, community forums, debating societies, and Town-Meetings-of-the-Air will clear. There the tested consequences of putting parts of the Master Designs into action will be appraised and revisions be made.

What Should National Government Do?

The current give-and-take of discussion of the problem has already precipitated a clearer view of the role to be played by the federal government. Five areas of positive dynamic leadership can now be discerned:

First: It must lead, as it has been doing so splendidly, in the creative positive process of research, study and design for social reconstruction. This means the continuation and marked expansion of Executive activities such as the NRPB and Congressional work like that of the TNEC. Here already is a great contribution to the improvement of American life.

Second: It must exhaust its imagination and energy in the positive stimulation of private enterprise to keep the national economic system running at full employment. This means especially such steps as the use of government finance and taxation agencies (1) to stimulate the free flow of credit to new and continuing enterprises—especially the smaller ones, and (2) to force investment of idle savings by "incentive taxation."

Third: It must be on a week-by-week alertness schedule appraising the success of these and similar measures. At the first indication of falling off in employment it should quickly interject large-scale social capital into the system. This may necessitate the creation of a whole system of Government Yardstick Corporations in each of the major areas of:

—Credit . . . government credit banks.

—Housing . . . a government housing corporation with resources vast enough really to prime the great construction enterprises of the country.

—Regional reconstruction corporations on the order of the TVA.

—Community reconstruction corporations.

—Government transportation, communication, and other public utilities corporations.

Who shall say how far the need will go?

Fourth: It must guarantee an abundant life commensurate with our national resources. It is the one agency in the country to lead in maintaining public morale. It can build confidence in every sector of the population. It has one direct and efficient way to do that. It can guarantee the security of the people: their investments, their jobs, their savings, their homes, their health, their old age. For example—government, as the central Voice of all the people, can tell every person with savings to invest: "Put your money to work in a sound constructive enterprise which will employ people and we'll stand back of your investment." It can tell every employable worker who is willing to work: "We guarantee you a job, either in private business or in one of our government enterprises." And to the few unwilling ones: "You shall not share in our abundant life unless you work." The government, through the President and the Executives in charge of the respective departments must speak, and keep speaking in no uncertain tones to every sector of the American people. Every one must feel its leading, confident stimulation and protection. Moreover, it must assume a function which central government in America has never been willing or able to take over: it must lead in a great nation-wide plan of education of the American people— the 80,000,000 grown-ups . . . the 20,000,000 youths between 16 and 24 . . . the 30,000,000 younger children. But more of that in Chapter VIII.

Fifth: It will continue to have negative regulative, punitive functions, but it must distinguish clearly where those lie. Let it supervise and investigate constantly . . . let it drive out and punish racketeering wherever it exists—whether in monopoly-capitalism or labor-crime. And let it regulate manifold phases of our high-powered social system, opening its mind to such hitherto unsupervised areas as the protection of small stockholders who have no control in management against exploitation by means of huge executive salaries and bonuses.

✓ ✓ ✓

Here then is the new Structure of Design Leadership sketching the outlines of a better life in abundant America.

Are the makings with which to produce in the next generation a golden age of abundance, democratic behavior, and integrity of expression available? They are indeed: natural resources . . . human resources . . . industrial resources . . . the experience of a three-hundred-year struggle of the people to accept and practice the democratic way of life . . . creative resources —artists and craftsmen, scientists, inventors, and experts in government, in industry and agriculture, in forestry and mining and research and planning institutions. The ingredients for a magnificent culture are at hand. That idea also the American people must know: that they can now gather together these makings of the Great Society and organize them into a national going concern that will bring forth on this continent the civilization of abundance, democracy, and beauty which is now potentially available.

This is the affirmation of the New Politics . . . the New Ethics . . . the New Esthetics . . . the New Education.

This is the Great Tradition speaking through the American Way.

There Is a New Song

In a world of muzzled nations, America speaks!

*Freed from the worship of classic alien forms, America
    speaks!*

*She speaks through her new government of good will and
        social engineering . . . through her House, her
        cultivated Valley . . .*
    *Through her own Poem, her own Theatre, her
        Dance, her Song.*

In this tragic moment in world history,
*In the midst of dire national danger . . . of bewilder-
    ment . . . of defeatism,*
Creative Americans are drawing the curtain aside
On a vista of world communal life
        *. . . of a civilization just over the horizon
        whose wealth, beauty and spirit*
*Will stagger the imagination and dwarf anything that has
    gone before.*

THE MOST CREATIVE MOMENT:
THE AMERICAN INSTATES
THE GREAT TRADITION

When Van Wyck Brooks wrote *America's Coming of Age* and Randolph Rourne *The Twilight of Idols* a quarter century ago, they found our leaders sadly wanting . . . in poetry and religion . . . competent only in pragmatic technical control. But in this tragic second phase of the Thirty Years War our cultural armament is quite different. Today America has both poetry and pragmatism . . . religion and efficient technology . . . and both are needed. Not only is this our moment because a free world of full employment-at-abundance-level can be established. It is actually the moment in which American creatives are nourishing the roots of the Great Tradition on our continent.

I think of Henry Wallace and his "People's Revolution" . . . of Harry Hopkins and his public works . . . of the NRPB and the Design Group in Washington . . . of Hugh Bennett and a generation of land reconstruction . . . of Harcourt Morgan, David Lilienthal, and their

associates cultivating That Valley . . . of Hallie Flanagan with her makings of a National Theatre—I think of
them as the first clear proof that the Great Tradition
could flower here now. There is in them the poetic religious idealization of the good life that could be lived
here now. There's poetry and religion in Henry Wallace's "century of the common man." There's the religious humility of the great gift in our leaders' chorus of
affirmation that we shall bind up the wounds of a sick
society! America, in selling of her riches to give to the
world, will be making far more than a formal gesture—
in a sense she will be holding church around the world.
There's love and idealization in Milo Perkins' "The plain
people of this earth . . . want to be wanted"; the voice
of an Answerer in his "The chains of the ages have
snapped." There's more than pragmatism in John
Winant's peace vision—"The drive for tanks must become the drive for houses." Alvin Hansen's "A people
can afford whatever it can produce" is both principle
and chant.

The Greatest Poems Are Being Written

You tell me I have idealized them,
Built up poetry where pragmatism is called for.

All right . . . it's poetry . . .
But it's poetry that is called for.
   Poetry can lift the world;
   Pragmatism can only direct it . . .
Both are needed . . . Both, praise be, are at hand.
Men of vision . . . Men of technical competence.

Only . . . don't belittle poetry
   or you'll be left . . .

Well structured, well aimed . . . with no engine force . . . Inert.

THE GREAT TRADITION IN THREE STAGES OF AMERICAN STATEMENT

If the American would be convinced that his people now have the makings of a sufficient philosophy, poetry, and religion let him study the lives and utterances of his fellow countrymen who have begun to produce them. Let him study the history of the creative act in North America. It is one of the major themes of my work that in the past century a dozen heroic Americans succeeded in laying the groundwork for the reinstatement of the Great Tradition. In my few remaining pages I cannot possibly give a full report of the manner in which this was achieved, but I shall attempt to present a convincing cross section of examples.

To do this, it will be helpful to visualize our moment as the third of three stages of cultural and expressive development through which our country in company with the other new ones, has been passing: First—transplantation from the mother culture. Second—rebellion and the appearance of partially indigenous improvisations. Third —creative and mature native expression.

First Stage: The Prolonged Thwarting of the Spirit of the Great Tradition

During the first stage, the 250-year-long period following the establishment of the original settlements, our cultural norms were almost entirely imported from Europe and Britain. As Emerson complained in the 1830s, we got our language, our letters, our arts, our customs and standards of thought from England. And Whitman in 1870 in *Democratic Vistas* pled for "a class of native authors . . . permeating the whole mass of American mentality, taste, belief, breathing into it a new breath of life." Yet despite their heroic efforts and the attempts of many authentic representatives of our cultural soil, the grip of the classic British-European tradition persisted.

It was in fact a tragic ordeal, for the creative worker had to struggle against three powerful hampering forces. The first was the raucous exploiting climate that encompassed the moving frontier of preëmption and settlement as it blazed its way across the continent. The second was the complete acceptance of classical culture with which cultivated people in the eastern cities taught their talented youth to follow the styles and standards of Britain and Europe. In every field of expression—in architecture, in letters, in the fine arts generally—almost nobody built, wrote, painted, or otherwise stated American life as it was really lived and in forms of original thought and feeling. Eclecticism and imitation were the order of the day. For two centuries almost every major creative American—poet, novelist, painter, what not—was satisfied to put down merely a prettified British-European version of his romantic dream-world of America.

The third psychological force that thwarted clear understanding and portraiture of life in America was the enslaving compression of false ideas—a curious fusion of animistic theology and mechanistic science. Even in the best of the new universities—for example, in Hopkins in the '80s and in Chicago in the '90s—only the rare malcontent—a Peirce, a Veblen, a Boas, a Thomas, was able to lift himself above the current theological interpretation of the universe.

Brought up in such a climate of opinion, most of the scientists and artists were content to deal with the superficies of life. Although in the 1880s and 1890s a few exceptional mutants did succeed in rising above the dead level of sheer exploitation, academic classicism, and imitative eclecticism, a great class of native authors was not born. In the superficial regime of the earlier period the merchant of art, architecture, and letters had ousted the creative artist. The poet and the playwright, the architect and the painter had to conform to the low esthetic standards of a thoroughly exploitive society.

THE VOICE OF "THE GREATEST POET"

But through it all there was one Voice sounding the American version of the Great Tradition. It was Walt Whitman who, almost alone from 1850 to 1890, withstood the lure of the classic mode and of imitation of European letters. In nine successive editions of *Leaves of Grass* he proclaimed that the poet makes the State while the politician exploits it with his intrigue and compacts and false regulations. He saw that a free creative society —which would be the Great Tradition on the grand scale —could emerge only in the fruition of a proud and self-conscious individualism—an individualism, however, that individualizes rather than exploits. The essence of society, distilled out of the new democratic melting pot, was to be full-bodied and full-minded selves. Whitman put it in the opening lines of *Leaves of Grass:*

> One's self I sing; a single separate person,
> Yet utter the word democratic.

But so full was the understanding of the organic thing in this great artist that the concept of a single living creature was comprehensive enough to embrace the whole organic world, including human society. The individuals together form the whole society—"a vast similitude interlocks all."

Second Stage: The Emergence of Native Creatives

Then, right after Whitman's death, the thing began to happen. The period of Expansion had passed, and the country whirled on into the Great Tradition—our own times. This exciting period manifested itself in two ways —in a vigorous revolt against the slavish conformity to classic norms and in a brilliant improvisation of new statements made directly and with increasing competence out of American life. Quite suddenly a thrilling band of creative Americans—architects and industrial designers, poets, novelists, painters, sculptors, men of the theatre, dancers, musicians, craftsmen, and social engineer-statesmen—was born.

I date the second stage from the 1890s—from the death of Whitman and the first indigenous portraits of Stephen Crane and Theodore Dreiser; from the first buildings of Louis Sullivan; from the first dances of Isadora Duncan; from the first social analyses of Thorstein Veblen and the New Historians; from William James's publicizing of his mistaken version of Charles Peirce's "pragmaticism"; from Alfred Stieglitz's first photographs of integrity.

These answerers and their successors are important; each in his respective medium forsook the stereotyped modes of imported European classic patterns and created an honest portrait of the American becoming conscious of his America. Each one—to the limits set by his own powers—shook off the circumscribing bonds of traditional art forms and created novel ones which were appropriate to his own images and ideas, true expressions of his own personal interpretations and conscious portraits of his America. No concept of living is more subtle than that one, or more difficult to achieve in a society in which competition and conformity are the standard ways of life. To make dramatically clear how that was done would require little less than a series of biographies of the artists themselves.

Third Stage: Mature Design and Execution

That we are well along in that second improvising stage of culture-development is shown by the fact that an impressive body of creative workers is already leading American expression into the third and more profound stage, and thus bringing the Great Tradition to life in our land. This is a regime of indigenous and original design and advancing maturity of statement.

On the social side, I know no better documentation than the exciting examples of the New Statesmanship of social engineering and welfare I have reported in the foregoing chapter.

In the medium of the House—perhaps the most universal mode of social as well as personal statement, certainly the one nearest to all the people—there were two true Answerers: the great forerunner, Louis Sullivan, and the Master Builder, Frank Lloyd Wright. Their story has been sketched in the chapter on The Valley and The

Cultivated Scene and I shall not dwell longer on them nor on Hugh Bennett, and David Lilienthal, and the cultivators of the land whose work is today eventuating in the continental restoration of the principle of the sustained-yield.

The Profile of the American Statement

To organize the many examples of profound achievement that illustrate this mature stage, I shall use a structural framework that I call the Profile of the American Statement. In the concept, "statement," I embrace the social-economic portraits and analyses of the scientific students of the culture as well as the novels, poems, essays, plays, houses, paintings, music, or dances of the artists. We shall not forget that while the scientific students were concentrating on "stating" the society, the artists were "stating" the Individual-becoming-Person who was living in it and also helping to rebuild it.

To clarify the meaning of "profile" think of shafts being sunk through successive "levels" or aspects of the culture of our people, as by analogy the earth scientist sinks similar ones through successive levels of topsoil, subsoil, gravel, hardpan, rock. At the surface of the culture are the folkways of the people, their daily doings and sayings and gestures. Beneath these are various submerged forces and factors: their human relations and ongoing group life and institutions . . . their social-economic-political-esthetic problems. There is the level of their uncritical mood—their passions and appreciations, their desires and taboos, fears and aspirations, hates and loves, and there is the level of their critical mind when intelligent appraisal is functioning. All of these phases of the life of the people partake of the dated localisms of men-in-this-time-and-place. There is however another, most foundational level of the culture, that is felt by only the most sensitive men; this is the level of Man-in-the-Universe-and-in-History.

It is obvious that profound utterances of expressive Americans must not, indeed cannot, be fitted arbitrarily into any set of categories. Any poem, novel, public address, play, dance, or painting may be a rigorous purposeful social document, and at the same moment seethe with spiritual passion; it may state searching generalizations and paint a cosmic panorama of truth, as well as portray character, sing lyrics, juxtapose personal human relationships, and sound the time-beat of circumscribed regional or national folkways. Nevertheless, a "profile" of this kind will help to focus thinking and to clarify the diffuse materials of the creative mind. I sum it up, therefore, in tabular form working "down" from the more obvious surface of the culture:

1. Statements of folkways and folklore.

2. Social documentation and problems of reconstruction, advancing sometimes into the universal or the cosmic.

3. Portraits of individual character, appraisals of human relationships, and such personal expression as lyrical utterance, love songs, and descriptive idyls, some of which rise into profound "hymns of being."

4. Critical analysis of the culture, of literary portraits of it and of methods of studying it . . . broadly conceived as "criticism."

5. The foundation of the profile, consisting of concepts of universal validity . . . Man-in-the-Universe-and-History

rather than men-in-this-time-and-place . . . the Great Tradition of the Person.

In every decade of our own Great Transition expressive Americans, employing every medium known to men, have been filling in these levels of the profile of the American statement. And now the record is a clear revelation that our adolescent exploitive culture is actually passing the threshold of a New Day.

I. Folk Statement

An important library of American folk statement began to take shape in the 1910s with the simple honest indigenous folk verse of Carl Sandburg sounding the time beat of mid-west prairie and city industrialism (from *Chicago Poems* to *The People, Yes*) . . . of Edgar Lee Masters' *Spoon River* epitaphs of small town life . . . of Vachel Lindsay's catching of the reverberations of farm and Negro life and Methodism—white and black . . . of the folk paintings of Thomas Benton, John Curry, and Grant Wood . . . of the folk theatre of George M. Cohan and long-run things like the recent *Tobacco Road, You Can't Take It With You, Life With Father, My Sister Eileen.*

To cite more spectacular current examples and to remind ourselves again of the contribution of government leadership in social reconstruction, witness the completion of the writing and publication of *The American Guide Series* (supplemented now by many smaller publications in *The American Life Series*). It is a spectacular contribution to the literature of American folkways.

II. Social Document

During the very years that the contours of these first folk portraits of the culture were being sketched, other creatives were digging below its surface to document its trends and problems and to outline the nature of its reconstruction. Convincing episodes of that pageant of moving history have already passed before our eyes—the building of the House and social reconstruction on the land . . . and the drawing of the first tentative designs for a post-war world of order and abundance. Perhaps others are not needed, but I cannot resist the brief citation of two—the magnificent social document that the FSA has produced in photography since 1934, and the emergence of several original documentary writing men.

Photography: A Social Document of American Life

Today America speaks through no more powerful medium of social expression than the science, technology, and social documentation of the photographer. Although her success in using the camera as an instrument of personal expression lags far behind this social achievement, its history is a striking illustration of the integration of the two. Side by side with the expressive artists a team of documentary photographers—Dorothea Lange, Russell Lee, Arthur Rothstein, Walker Evans, Paul Carter, Ben Shahn, Carl Mydans—have been making an organic social portrait of the ways of living and problems of our people in every region of the country.

One man, Roy Stryker—not a photographer but a social scientist—had the imagination to get this work done with government facilities. When Rex Tugwell and his associates were building up the Resettlement Administration, RA (now the Farm Security Administration, FSA), they organized a so-called Historical Section to develop methods of acquainting the American people with their actual rural conditions. Stryker, the Director—former cowboy, miner, soldier—had learned as Columbia colleague of and co-author with Tugwell how to portray American life through pictures. Until he went to Washington in 1933, the federal government had ignored the Brady Civil War pictures and comparable ones by the Bureau of Reclamation, Forest Service, and Extension Service.

After 1933 the Historical Section quickly built up a tremendous file of photographs "to reveal the state of the nation in terms of the land and the people" . . . "to show New Yorkers to Texans and Texans to New Yorkers . . . to show steel workers what a Louisiana sharecropper looks like, what kind of house he lives in, how he works, what he wears, how he plays, and the problems he's up against—so when a bill to aid sharecroppers is up before Congress and the Pennsylvania senators support the bill, the Pennsylvania voters will say 'O.K.' . . . The idea is to substitute understanding for machine guns and a Gestapo as a means of keeping the country working together, unified, coöperating." But Russell Lee says it is even more than that, "The Historical Section is accumulating a file of pictures which may endure to help the people of tomorrow understand the people of today, so they can carry on more intelligently."

A half dozen photographer-students of American culture, trekking through the Old South states . . .

through the mountain states and back across the middle west and into New England, have made a remarkable social document—simple and honest, unposed photographs —grim, because most of them were of "busted farmers and migrants, . . . tractored off the land." In 1939 Stryker got experts to appraise the output, and a fine sample was published in *U. S. Camera Annual* with an introduction by Edward Steichen.

America produces her first social novelists

A parallel body of documentary novels has accumulated since Edith Wharton's success with *The Age of Innocence* and Upton Sinclair's *Jungle* and other "homiletic" novels actually brought about governmental reforms of social life. Sinclair, internationally acclaimed for his fifty documentary novels, is currently "documenting" the problems of our times with the large Lanny Budd cycle. Sinclair Lewis ran his portraits of American communities, professions, and types in *Main Street, Babbitt, Arrowsmith*—to name the better ones. And out of twenty years of the Long Armistice America produced at least seven important social novelists: John Dos Passos, William Faulkner, Erskine Caldwell, Ernest Hemingway, Thomas Wolfe, James T. Farrell, and John Steinbeck. They are weaned of slavish conformity to expressional norms of the mother culture. They have gusto, imagination and the "individual touch"; they are skilled masters of composition; they all make lifelike portraits of the American scene, creating characters that live on in the reader's gallery of literary acquaintances—and they are genuinely typical of the social revolt, storm and stress, and changing loyalties of our times.

Meanwhile social documents have been coming from some of our poets. One thinks of our poet-in-government Archibald MacLeish for his *The Land of the Free* (with the magnificent photographic collaboration of Dorothea Lange, Russell Lee *et al.* of FSA) and *America Was Promises*. Although nothing has come from his pen recently, he has been much in the periodical prints, partly because of the recurring rebuttal to *The Irresponsibles* which criticized the "scholars" for their inertness in the current crisis, but primarily because of the acclaim of his administration of the Library of Congress and his influence on government and the American mind through his work with the Office of War Information. For the moment, poetry will lose a major writer—but what a preparation these two jobs (and almost daily attendance in the President's inner circle of advisors) are for documentary literature in the years ahead!

In the current output of social poetry there is Paul Engle's *American Song* and *West of Midnight;* Robinson Jeffers' various epic poems, including the long Hitler piece "Bowl of Blood"; profound social things from Robert Frost like his "Build Soil." There are many others on the documentary level . . . but these few typify the best.

III. PERSONAL STATEMENT

If one digs still further down into the culture he finds an overwhelming body of personal expression in every medium. The poet, the novelist, the dancer, the composer, the painter—each is beginning to state his life in America as he sees it in his own unique way. A superb example of this level of the culture—already described in detail in Chapter II—is the achievement of man building his house, building it for the life to be lived in it.

The bare statistical record of the poets since the turn of the century is nothing short of amazing—and a good percentage of it is fine lyrical utterance. In the spirit of the clear Voice of the pioneer Emily Dickinson many of our poets have caught that timeless quality of a people growing sensitive to universals: Sara Teasdale in her eloquent volumes containing such flawless polished lyrics as "Morning," "The Song Maker," "Night Song at Amalfi," "Water Lilies," "Let it be Forgotten," and "The Solitary"; Edna St. Vincent Millay in her rich contribution ranging all the way from the momentary "Figs from Thistles" to the rare mastery of "God's World," "Renascence," and "Euclid alone has looked on Beauty bare"; Elinor Wylie in her sophisticated "Incantation," "Escape," "Wild Peaches," and "Castilian"; Marianne Moore in "Poetry" and "The Monkeys." Other fine examples have come from Adelaide Crapsey, the two Benets— William Rose and Stephen Vincent, Witter Bynner, John Hall Wheelock, Louise Bogan, Ezra Pound, T. S. Eliot, Hart Crane, Robinson Jeffers, and William Carlos Williams.

Personal expression in the form of the appraisal of human relationships, the evaluation of personalities and their impact on the culture is found in the constantly growing body of first rank autobiographies and biographies of Americans. Other significant character portrayal and personal expression are found in novels such as Waldo Frank's *The Death and Birth of David Markand*, *The Bridegroom Cometh*, *City Block*, *Chalk Face* . . . John Steinbeck's *Tortilla Flat* . . . Vardis Fisher's tetralogy on the Snake River region in Idaho . . . William Faulkner's continuing saga of a Mississippi town . . . Thomas Wolfe's *Look Homeward Angel* . . . Ernest Hemingway's *A Farewell to Arms* and *For Whom the Bell Tolls* . . . and Christopher LaFarge's novel in verse, *Each to the Other*.

In the movement arts a comparable sensitive record has been built by fifty years of honest lyric utterance in the dance since Isadora Duncan and Ruth St. Denis first made their statements—now exemplified by Martha Graham, Doris Humphrey, and other contemporaries . . . and by the parallel achievement of the musicians writing in the framework of the personal reference of the dancer —Wallingford Riegger, Henry Cowell, Louis Horst, and George Anteil.

There is also the playwright's record of sensitive portrayals of human relationships of which plays like Eugene O'Neill's *Strange Interlude*, *Anna Christie*, *Beyond the Horizon* . . . William Saroyan's *The Beautiful People*, *My Heart's in the Highlands*, *The Time of Your Life* . . . and Steinbeck's *Of Mice and Men* are outstanding examples.

The painters of the Great Transition group—Robert Henri, Arthur B. Davies, and "The Eight"—can be traced from three Victorian forerunners—Albert Ryder, Winslow Homer, Thomas Eakins. Out of their period of improvisation of American forms emerged hundreds of original painters, with John Marin, Eugene Speicher, Henry McFee, Georgia O'Keeffe, and Henry Mattson in the vanguard.

In this brief cataloguing of names and works on the level of personal expression the reader can sense the richness and variety with which creative Americans of the Great Transition are making their personal statement.

IV. THE INGREDIENTS OF A GREAT CRITICISM

That America reveals both pragmatism and poetry and that both are competent to deal with the staggering problems of today is shown perhaps best of all by the work that has been done on the critical level of our profile. For a half century a distinguished body of "critics" has produced a scholarly analysis and appraisal of industrial-democratic culture. I use the term "critics" not in the narrow sense conventionally employed in the arts alone, but to embrace all who consciously strive to analyze the deepest roots and traits of the society. This means a three-fold company of social philosophers, social scientists, and social estheticians. I accent the "social" because all these critics did so—in literature, painting and sculpture, theatre, music, dance, architecture, and industrial design as well as in community and national reconstruction. Since *The Seven Arts* and Van Wyck Brooks' epoch-marking *America's Coming of Age* (1915), esthetic statements have been appraised as much for their cultural indigenousness as for the extent to which they achieve organic form.

Four Creative Frontiers

At the time of Whitman's death distinguished groups of Americans on several stirring creative frontiers were assaying and nourishing the roots of the Great Tradition in American life. Today, fifty years later, every vestige of the former menial clinging to the classic standard forms of utterance has disappeared.

On the *social frontier* Charles Peirce, William James, and the philosophers . . . Thorstein Veblen, Frederick Turner, and the new historians, economists and political scientists . . . William Thomas, Franz Boas, Ellsworth Huntington, and the sociologists, anthropologists, social psychologists, and regional geographers have slowly been documenting and clarifying new concepts of the social scene: the organic nature of experience . . . the role of generalization, of relationship, in thinking . . . the nature of growth in the living creature . . . the totality of "the culture" as the process of interaction of dynamic individuals and the impact of physical and social environments and human modes of living upon one another . . . the unified interrelationship of economics, politics, and social psychology.

✔ ✔ ✔

On the *personal frontier* were similar groups of scientific students of the living creature—the students of evolution . . . Walter B. Cannon and the laboratory physiologists . . . William James, John Dewey, and the students of animal and human psychology. They were documenting such concepts of organic life as: things growing from small beginnings . . . the generalized nature of the growth of living creatures . . . the central role of the perception of relationships and generalizations in learning and behavior.

✔ ✔ ✔

On the *esthetic frontier*, working concurrently with the others, slowly formed a fine group of workers in the creative arts: poets, novelists, literary and social critics, architects and industrial designers, painters, sculptors, men of the theatre, dancers, musicians. Steadily they assembled more ingredients that would instate the Great Tradition from the soil of American life, learning to stand alone as expressive artists . . . to make their own statements of American life as they saw it in their own unique ways . . . as they became increasingly articulate about the concept necessary to that statement. In fifty years of hard work Sullivan and Wright . . . Duncan, Graham, and Company . . . Frank and the new literary critics . . . O'Neill, Jones, Cheney of the new theatre— to name only a few—groped their way through to a modern statement of the great principle of organic form —with its clarifying criteria of functionality . . . economy . . . and the related elements of organization. Their life work came to stand for a new integrity of expression.

One of the most important exhibits of our new cultural independence was the emergence of a score of "little reviews"—magazines of criticism in the decade and a half following 1910. I speak briefly of only one, *The Seven Arts,* founded in 1916 by Waldo Frank and James Oppenheim and associates. First and foremost it was an organ of social criticism. Its editors were creative, imaginative painters of American life. These clear and honest students laid bare the vicious commercialism of the arts; they showed how impossible it is for great art to thrive in a profiteering, racketeering climate; they exposed the widespread mode of imitation of European and classic forms in letters, the stage, music and the dance, architecture, and the graphic and plastic arts; they laid the foundations for an original critique of the current pragmatic philosophy of James and Dewey; they revealed the disappearing loyalties of modern peoples, pointing out that ours was a society of lost individuals; they stated the concepts of a new philosophy which could be built directly out of the data of American life, showed the necessity of seeing life whole, and antedated the current educational interpretation of integration.

✓   ✓   ✓

Coincidentally on a fourth *frontier of education*—a group of creative workers with children and youth were rediscovering the educative processes involved in the instatement of the Great Tradition. Many among them were true *artist*-teachers, each one a master of some medium of expression and sensitive to the devolpment of the creative act in other people. The first to make himself felt was Colonel Francis W. Parker through his revolutionary experiments in child-centered education at Quincy, Massachusetts (1875-1880) and at the Chicago Normal School (1883-1901); second came Mr. and Mrs. John Dewey and their famous Laboratory School at the University of Chicago (1896-1904); third there were J. L. Meriam and his experimental school at the University of Missouri in the years following 1904. Then after a pause of several years a score of "new," "experimental" schools were set up by progressive parents and teachers; enough indeed so that by the winter of 1918-1919 the fine nucleus could form the Progressive Education Association. In these schools, especially after the middle 1920s, a whole new organized creative education was slowly developed around the organic point of view and concepts that the workers on the other frontiers had unearthed.

✓   ✓   ✓

Thus as our country passed into the explosive era of the

Great Transition, creative Americans were studying their culture on several broad frontiers. For a half century they struggled with problems of imagination and documentation. Using the two great methods of Man-as-Orderer they worked both as intuitive artists in the framework of their personal life orientations and as documenting scientists, critically studying every aspect of American life. Looking back on it we can today chant with Whitman and Sullivan "thus widened the Democratic Vista." There opened to view a period of brilliant improvisation and increasingly sensitive design of indigenous houses, poems, plays, dances, schools, socially reconstructed valleys, and social-engineering-welfare government. It seemed that at last the Great Tradition was coming to life on the North American continent.

V. Man-in-the-Universe-and-in-History: The Roots of the Great Tradition

If these native improvisations are to flower into maturity they must be nourished in the rich earth of philosophy and religion. We cannot escape measuring ourselves on Waldo Frank's criterion: "No adequate politics, no adequate ethics, no adequate esthetics without an adequate metaphysic and social religion." Our creative leaders must become articulate in answering such questions as:

What kind of man do we envisage in our special American brand of democratic society?

What kind of life will be called Good . . . will be called Moral?

On what does morality in our industrial society rest?

What is knowledge?

How does man know?

What is the role of the report of the separate senses . . . their integration in the organism's total intuition?

To what extent does knowledge determine morality . . . and thereby the Good Society?

Although it has been traditional with us to assign the leadership in this sphere of creative thought to the ordained secular and religious philosophers, other creative workers have an equal claim to the title of "philosopher." When, for example, a great Answerer of the House like Frank Lloyd Wright, creates a design for a Broadacre community and founds it upon a phrased philosophy of American life, he is serving as a philosopher. And when Walt Whitman states the role of the Greatest Poet and thereby precipitates a religion of humanity which will serve as the foundation of true democracy, he is philosopher and religionist as well as poet. A critic of the culture who digs to its religious roots, as does Waldo Frank in *America Hispana . . . Virgin Spain . . . Rediscovery of America . . .* and *Chart for Rough Water*, must be listened to as philosopher and man of religion, as well as novelist and literary critic.

✓ ✓ ✓

As a layman, I must disclaim any pretension to do more than state in outline form the problem of building an adequate metaphysic and social religion. I shall try to sketch the conditions in the culture that predetermined the limits of achievement in the past three generations . . . and to characterize succinctly the nature of the philosophic and religious foundation which they succeeded in constructing.

Two important psychological forces molded the men and their work. The first, emanating from the premonitory year of 1859—the date of *Origin of Species*—was the grip of science on the minds of professed philosophers, ministers of the churches, students of the new social sciences, and captains of industry. The sixties and seventies were a stormy period of intellectual and emotional controversy over Darwin's hypotheses. It is not too much to say that the nub of intellectual stimulation of the decades immediately following the Civil War lay in the evolutionary concepts and the scientific climate of opinion which radiated swiftly out from the maturing physical sciences and mechanical technologies.

This condition motivated the second psychological force, namely the raucous mood of settlement and exploitation of the land. The chief concepts hurled against men's minds by the hectic din of construction were: conquer . . . preëmpt and clear the land . . . build quickly the structure of civilization; as one poet expressed it, "bigness and be-damnedness" . . . and as every one of the buccaneering builders exclaimed almost daily, "I'll be rich!" It was Manifest Destiny on the march. The inevitable result of the swift unplanned setting up of power-machine-factory-production and the consequent rise of industrial cities, specialization of labor, and the regimentation of work and life was that millions of city inhabitants lived in squalor, ill health, anxiety, and fatigue.

Baldly confronted by such widespread misery, intensified by the juxtaposition of Gold Coasts and Slums, most of the socially conscious men of thought and religious feeling could do little more in the years of industrial expansion than commit themselves either to the intellectual rationalization of the great technology or to social reform. In doing so they voiced the Center-to-Left of the Great Tradition in the struggle against Center-to-Right of the Exploiters.

THE "GOSPEL OF WEALTH" OF THE CENTER-TO-RIGHT

The intellectual and religious leaders of the Center-to-Right—such Fundamentalist college presidents as Noah Porter of Yale, James McCosh of Princeton, and Mark Hopkins of Williams—really the mouthpieces for the successful masters of industrial and financial capitalism—developed the ruling philosophy of the colleges, universities, and churches. It was a nominalist, "divine right" philosophy of property rights. As Professor Paul Elmer More put it as late as the turn of the century: "Looking at the larger good of society, we may say that the dollar is more than the man and that the rights of property are more important than the right to life." The church element in this movement was exemplified by the Fundamentalists and such leaders as the popular Baptist clergyman and platform lecturer, Russell H. Conwell, who gave his "rugged individualism" lecture—"Acres of Diamonds"—6000 times to approving middle-class audiences.

Their chief intellectual concept, following Andrew Carnegie's own autobiographical rationalization of the behavior of the masters of capital, was what became widely known as the Gospel of Wealth. Offspring of a half dozen generations of Puritanism, it taught in sermon, lecture, and textbook the obligation of each American to work hard to own property, and to protect it for moral ends. Carnegie's secular form of it was four-fold: individualism, private property, and the "laws" of accumulation of wealth and of competition. He preached for his "Capitalist Utopia" the Darwinian concept of the survival of the fittest, "the strong shall inherit the earth," and the concept of "stewardship"—that is, the obligation of charity. The pursuit of wealth for itself was considered ignoble, but as a means to social ends it could become "a glorious adventure."

PRAGMATISM AND THE SOCIAL GOSPEL OF THE CENTER-TO-LEFT

While the Fundamentalists were proclaiming a Gospel of Wealth a two-fold movement was developing on the Center-to-Left: pragmatism in the colleges, and a secular "religion of humanity," that has come to be known generally as the Social Gospel, in the churches. The Social Gospel constituted an aggressive humanism; it was formulated in the combined framework of the democratic idea and the Christian gospel of the brotherhood of man, with emphasis on social reform. Here was the characteristic approach to the Great Tradition that revealed itself in the academic and religious culture.

The chief secular foundation stone of the Social Gospel was the method of findings of science, especially the new anthropology which had grown out of Comte's conception of the three stages of man's progress. A rigorous new determinism developed under the leadership of such students as Lewis Henry Morgan, author of *Ancient Society*, and John Wesley Powell, organizer of the United States Geological Survey, "high priest of the cult of the science of man."

Massachusetts was the center of preachment of reform and distinguished names headed the roster. On the philosophical side: Ralph Waldo Emerson, Francis E. Abbott, William Lloyd Garrison the younger, Thomas Wentworth Higginson, Wendell Phillips, and Bronson Alcott —the leaders of the Boston Radical Club. On the more strictly religious side: Octavius B. Frothingham, first president of the Free Religious Association . . . Jesse H. Jones, Congregational minister who formed the Christian Labor Union in 1872 . . . Robert H. Ingersoll, "the great heretic"—independent preacher of skepticism and greatest orator of the 1880s and 1890s . . . Washington Gladden, national crusader for a new, rather middle-of-the-road liberalism . . . William D. P. Bliss and the fiery, unconventional Congregational minister George D. Herron, who, influenced by Henry George and George Bellamy, gave impetus to Christian socialism. Siding fearlessly with labor, they advocated collective bargaining, coöperative banks, stores, and workshops, warned of the danger of the break-up of industrial civilization, and sought to find the uniting principle that would hold the people together in a fusion of liberal secular principles of a modernized religion of the brotherhood of man.

Their work came to the dignified level of intellectual organization in the hands of Walter Rauschenbusch, a church historian. Influenced by his mission work with the poor on the east side of New York City, he gave the Social Gospel movement a solid historical and intellectual foundation in three memorable books: *Christianity and the Social Crisis* (1907) . . . *Christianizing the Social Order* (1912) . . . and *A Theology for the Social Gospel* (1917). A year after his first book appeared, the

Federal Council of Churches of Christ in America was organized and this has proved to be a real force in the Social Gospel movement. It has supported the progressive efforts of labor and emphasized the implementation of theology in the social problems of the day. Thus the Federal Council committed itself to a kind of secular progressivism, demanding that "social justice be defined in Christian terms."

The leadership in the attempt to reconstruct Protestant theology around the concept of social justice fell to Rauschenbusch. He attacked the evils of industrial capitalism, including competition, monopoly, useless middlemen, and the profit motive. "Business," he said, "is the last intrenchment of autocracy, and wherever democracy is beaten back, the sally is made from that citadel." He lined up with the farm populists, attacking the exploiting role of the middlemen and criticizing the profit motive as "tribute collected by power from the helpers." Christianity, he said, could never be content with such a "mammonistic organization as industrial capitalism."

He appraised the church in the light of its long history and outlined a theology around the concept of a society in which the moral law is really the foundation of a social ethics. This would never come about until we abolish unjust privilege, and this could be done only by much socialization of property, not communism, but the American two-fold way of social and private capital in coöperation. Rauschenbusch's theology, therefore, was built around the concept of "the Kingdom of God" on earth, which he defined as "an historical force . . . a vital and organizing energy now at work in humanity." The fundamental "law" of human society is love and this is incompatible with capitalism, war, competition, or monopoly. This moral and theological law is also the foundation of democracy, and the Kingdom of God is its highest expression. Thus the brotherhood of man has a theological basis and the real mission of the Social Gospel is to "put the democratic spirit which the church inherited from Jesus and the prophets once more in control of the institutions and teachings of the church."

Hence the Social Gospel consisted of a secularization of the religious temper; the pulpit became a lay rostrum. Its powerful instrument was the "community church" which, in the hands of a fine succession of preachers from Octavius B. Frothingham to John Haynes Holmes, became the "church of the unchurched." It was a Center-to-Left expression and constituted a progressive reaching out for the instatement of the Great Tradition.

A PRAGMATIC PHILOSOPHY FOR A SENSATE CULTURE

So much for the men of religion. What was happening on the frontier of secular philosophy? A totally new dynamic thing. As the United States came out of the Civil War and started west to complete the conquest of the continent, it could be said fairly that the intellectuals of the young nation had no phrased philosophy. Neither was there an organized profession of American philosophers. Fifty years later when we entered the first phase of the World War, all that was changed. The new industrial capitalism had produced scores of professed philosophers and most of them did their thinking and program-making in the general outlook known variously as "pragmatism" or "empiricism" . . . "instrumentalism" . . . "operationalism," or even on occasions as "positivism."

This, I am confident, was historically inevitable. In an ultra-sensate society the practical high-speed and technological climate of opinion was bound to rationalize itself in an utilitarian, instrumental, and quantitative philosophy. Study the lives and works of the three leaders who phrased this orientation—Charles Sanders Peirce, William James, and John Dewey—and the case becomes convincing.

Although there are sharp differences between Peirce and Dewey on the one hand, and James on the other, for our purposes we can link them together. They and their disciples all committed themselves to the social emphasis, to the emerging American brand of democracy, and to the concepts and methods of science—in the human sciences to the Darwinian idea. Peirce was one of the world's most distinguished mathematical physicists and logicians . . . thirty years on the United States Coast and Geodetic Survey . . . world renowned for his original contributions in exact measurement, mathematics, and statistics. Today many accept Josiah Royce's estimate that he was the most original mind on the North American continent in the nineteenth century. William James, Peirce's baffled admiring friend, was more "artist" than scientist . . . distinguished empiric, more-or-less-unwilling builder of the first psychological laboratory in the United States . . . the first to reflect the practical, active, organizing climate of the American man-on-the-street in the psychology and philosophy. John Dewey, in the first quarter of the twentieth century, made the world's most distinguished contribution to the description of "the experimental method of knowing." He clarified a half dozen foundational concepts: "thinking as problem solving" . . . "meaning and knowing arising through active response and through the testing of consequences" . . . "the unity of experience; that is, that ends and means, motive and act, will and deed are continuous" . . . "experience as the interaction of individuals" . . . "psychology as social psychology" . . . and society and its education of all-the-children-of-all-the-people conceived as a democracy built on the foregoing ideas.

The making of the pragmatic statement was a first-rank achievement in the history of creative thought. The pragmatists succeeded in stating in the short space of fifty years the scientific method of thought and work—one of Man-the-Orderer's two profound methods of organization. I agree emphatically with the estimate of my colleague Professor John Childs, that this is a "profoundly important development in the ethical life of the race" and that we should "resist all efforts, no matter how well intentioned, to supplant it by an authoritarian or by a purely personal arbitrary procedure."

Peirce, and to a limited extent, some of his younger followers, as well as such distinguished free-lance contemporaries as James Feibleman, succeeded in building on the new dynamic psychology the outlines of what could become foundational "realist" philosophy of man-in-the-universe-and-in-history. But for most of the pragmatic experimentalists the achievement is one of psychology rather than philosophy. Pragmatism, as viewed in fifty years of history, is essentially the psychological basis of humanism. As Peirce said straight out in his original articles in 1879-80, "How We Make Our Ideas Clear," it gave itself primarily to clarifying questions of how we think, how we form concepts, fix beliefs, and solve problems. It was a major contribution of distinguished creative minds to the building of an efficient, practicable psychology of democracy.

Toward the Great Myth of Modern Man

It is clear, therefore, that creative effort on the part of the Center-to-Left in philosophy and religion from the Civil War to the Great Depression left us with little more than a vigorous American humanism. As I said earlier, "well structured . . . well aimed . . . but with little engine force." Then the pendulum swung back. In the framework of reaction against the extremes of the revolt and improvisation of the New Freedom of the twenties, sensitive men-as-artists protested the inadequacy of pragmatism in secular philosophy and the more thoughtful churchmen began to question the adequacy of the Social Gospel. As for the latter, in the more conservative centers the reaction took the form of an emphatic return to Fundamentalist theology. But in the liberal seminaries also, young ministers and professors increasingly expressed their fears that "the sociology of the Christian message was false to its historic character." A vigorous trend set in, not for "the return to" but for "the recovery of" theology, that is, a powerful emotionalized body of moving doctrine or belief. A new group of social liberals, led by such professors of religion and education as Reinhold Niebuhr, Paul Tillich, and F. Ernest Johnson, while accepting the concepts of science, evolution, and social justice, criticized the religious shallowness of the Social Gospel movement. As one young minister said, "The message of our society is not enough . . . it has missed the real message of the Kingdom of God." Or, as Professor Johnson has recently expressed it, "Our liberal social Christianity needs to rediscover its roots in the Christian faith."

What are these roots? The most profound current answers are being given by those who are struggling to recover the emotional doctrinal power of religion that inheres in a true theology. Modern men will be persuaded to fight to the death for the Great Tradition (the Supreme Value of the Individual) only if they come to feel that their dearest spiritual possessions are at stake. As Johnson says, the Social Gospel (and I know he would add with me—pragmatism) merely gave us intellectual "conclusions"—generalizations drawn from the documented data of the new society. And I agree with him and the New Orthodoxists that men will not die for generalizations. But they will die for doctrines, for dogmas, for beliefs which spring from the deepest emotions of their lives.

It was inevitable that in our young sensate society, now passing through its first great transitional day, we would have momentarily lost the basic religious concepts, would have been caught by the intriguing problems of intellectual rationalization. But now that time has passed; we are confronted by world-wide tragedy and we are compelled to search the very foundations of our culture for possible resources in our great crisis. Especially should we ask what man-in-history has to teach us. What was it, for example, that held together the harassed peoples of earlier crisis epochs? I agree with Professor Niebuhr that the great religious myth constituted the driving emotional force. The Hebraic-Christian tradition was the longest continuous religious movement of mankind and, chiefly because of its mythical heritage, survived a succession of cultural revolutions that bordered on catastrophe. Niebuhr, Frank, *et al.* point to the experience of the Jews and the early Christians under Isaiah, Amos, Jesus, and others, each of whom developed and built up great religious culture-myths which unified the people and gave them the power to endure privation and oppression and, though caught in deep tragedy, to maintain their culture.

I am convinced, therefore, that in the classic culture-myth we have an important cue to aid us in our present extremity. Today, hundreds of thinking Americans are saying: "We must make a religion of democracy." To do so we càn make use of the powerful constellation of ideas in the American version of the Supreme Value of the Individual. Our three-century moving frontier has already served to emotionalize this pattern somewhat—but it is still inert . . . it is still little more than a humanistic idea. It needs to be suffused with a driving emotion, to be turned into tenacious belief, raised to the obsession of desire. In short, into a great modern people's Myth.

The myth, as Niebuhr and company remind us, is supra-scientific . . . more than intellectually factual. It has all the propulsive power of Belief . . . Dogma . . . Doctrine. It "alone is capable of picturing the world as a realm of coherence and meaning which defies the facts of incoherence." And that is exactly what we need most today. Although our scientific documenting brains tell us that the interdependence, complexity, and chaos of our world is too great for men to master it, our Myth will affirm that if we want it with burning desire and know it with unalterable belief we can turn our warring world into one of practical coöperation and abundance. But we'll never do it unless we believe it in our bones. Man beaten down and on his knees is fumbling for hidden reservoirs of power with which to coil his muscles and build his new world. He must know and know that, as in the Hebraic prophetic days, so today "a genuine faith in transcendence" can be generated in the people. This deep emotion will literally "make a religion out of democracy," lift us above the current fearsome impasse in the culture and expand the American Way into the new World Way—the great Myth of modern man—of abundance and security.

THE MAKINGS OF THE GREAT MYTH

We come then to two questions: What ingredients are at hand to supply the content of a great people's Myth? Where are they to be found? That is, which country has the greatest potentiality for leading the world out of its slough of despond?

The full answer to the first question could engage the total effort of our secular and religious philosophers (the "profane" as well as "sacred" ones) for many years to come, and the need at this moment is so critical that much of their energy should be focused on it now.[1] Lacking their fuller answer, the layman certainly cannot pretend to make a rounded statement of the makings of the Great Myth. Nevertheless some of its conceptual facets are clear even now and these I shall mention briefly.

I find the very heart of it in the cumulating social experience of western man, especially in the practical im-

---

[1] From the references in my earlier chapters it is evident that persons like W. T. Stace, James Feibleman, and Waldo Frank are fully aware of that.

plementation of the idea of the Supreme Value of the Individual—his dignity and worth . . . his freedoms . . . his equalities . . . his expression . . . and his communal relationships as a potential Person. As I indicated in preceding chapters, the general concepts of the freedoms, the equalities, the brotherhood of man that were written into charters of liberty are now, in our revolutionary times, being suffused with energizing color. Witness how the democratic peoples are now demanding the realization of those ideas: the augmenting chorus of the people who "want to be wanted" . . . who insist on wiping out the political, economic, and social forms of the color-line . . . the mood rising to crescendo across America that India must be freed now, asking that the word "all" in "all men are created equal" be given real meaning . . . eminent British leaders demanding the drastic reconstruction of the social system . . . erstwhile business leaders like Wendell Willkie favoring the disinterested humanitarianism of the more profound statesmanship.

Moreover, two great concepts that a few years ago were only the intellectual conclusions of the students of society, have already become the chief slogans of government planners. I mean, first, the idea that a people can afford whatever it can produce, and second, the enforced unity of mankind—hitherto the dream of Utopians,—but now pragmatically sanctioned by modern man's technological mastery of the production of goods and services and the consequent interdependence of all industrialized populations. These ideas seem to me to be important constituents out of which the Great Myth may be generated in the coming years.

That brings us to the second question, which takes us

even more than before out of the realm of mere interpretation and to the verge of prediction: Where will these makings of the Great Myth most likely be found at the cessation of hostilities? Which of the four allies—America, Britain, Russia, China—will stand in the strategic position of leadership in world reconstruction? For a full answer we must wait for the revelations of trend and the clarification of several unknowns. There are several large "ifs," for example:

Which British government will be in power during the armistices—the present Churchill "Toryish" one? A Cripps liberal-Laborite one? A thorough-going "social-reconstructionist" one?

How physically strong and assertive of its philosophy will Russia be? China? The smaller nations?

How united will the Americans be? Which government will be in power—the present full-employment-world-rehabilitation, Center-to-Left one, or one from the Center-to-Right?

Confronted by these gigantic "ifs" who can foresee the personnel of power and leadership two, three, four years hence? No single layman certainly. Yet each of us engaged in studying the scene is obligated, it seems to me, to bring forward the results of his best thinking and prevision, even if it be no more than a general integration of his feeling, his reaction to the advancing social trend and temper. I'll rush in this far then:

First, physical power. At the coming of the armistices the United States will occupy by far the most strategic position for leadership in world reconstruction. She will have tremendous superiority in physical accumulation of war materials and world-wide air and sea transport facilities, in potential financial capacity and actual developed domestic production plant.

Second, transcending emotional power. Of all the brands of "democracy" that western Europe and her satellite civilizations have developed in the past several hundred years, there seems to me to be more potential transcending power in the American brand than in any other. Compare, from the single standpoint of "classlessness," the varieties of democracy in the thirty-odd countries where it has had some chance to evolve, especially since 1600 A.D., notably the British Commonwealth of Nations, Scandinavia, France, and Latin America. From the experience of actual residence in all these except the South American countries, has come the deep impress upon my mind of populations, which, in spite of their abolition of royalty and titles, and the liberalization of their Constitutions, were still "class" societies.

In utter humility and with the deepest respect for the heroic efforts of democratic leaders around the entire earth, I am convinced that in our own beloved land lies the nearest approximation to the "classless" society—to a social order in which the Supreme Value of the Individual receives its greatest nourishment. I have recognized bluntly and have grimly documented in earlier chapters the nasty cleavages between our Center-to-Right and Center-to-Left. I grant the horrid outcome of man's inhumanity to man in America during the First Industrial Revolution, and have shown how the Exploitive Tradition ran its course on our continent as destructively as elsewhere on man's earth. And yet, at the very moment of picturing the raggedly anemic and ugly outcomes of our urban and agrarian history as well as the ruggedly strong and beautiful ones, I hold that the true spirit of "classlessness"—potential brotherhood of man— has been carried further here than anywhere on earth. I find it in our tenacious affirmation of the equality of the laborer and the dignity of labor . . . in the concept of the ladder-of-opportunity-open-to-all so that each may rise to the highest stature of which he is capable . . . in the great two-fold concept of I and We: The Bill of Rights and the Bill of Duties—the "keep off each other and keep each other off" associated with the sense of "we must do it together." I hold that while America is puzzled, ignorant, and bewildered, uncertain of problems, factors, or solutions, and is governed by much wishful thinking, yet there is "in the average American a profound humbleness; a hunger to do the things together in some way is still alive in us." I believe, therefore, that the historic mood of the Americans generalized for more of the world in the next few years, will go far toward determining the goals held before mankind—whether they be marked by the spirit of confidence or of pessimism, humanitarianism, or vengeance. The logic of this book has argued that the Americans have the makings for the great Myth of modern man. Here lie the springs of the tremendous emotion needed to supply the lifting power with which to push the social world back on to the path of the Great Tradition.

It would be easy to say, with Professor Niebuhr and the new theology, that this emotion is Love. Eventually, yes, it will be love of fellow man that will most perfectly make the Two Men . . . One . . . that will reconcile I and We . . . that will fuse practical enlightened self-interest with a profound humanitarianism. But the key group of American social engineers, now struggling to found their new politics, ethics, esthetics, and education on an adequate metaphysic and religion, are practical men as well as idealists. They know that even the present crucible of Armageddon will not burn all the Exploitive Tradition out of competitive man. With Madariaga they will be content, for our generation, if we take the first step—and they hope it will be a major stride—"toward virtue." I think that if our social-engineering government can be kept in power it will lead our people in making the great gesture toward the Great Tradition. That will be that first stride—not far, perhaps, from Love itself.

All the factors, then, seem to proclaim that this is the favored moment: the tragic depth of the crisis . . . the exhaustion of every major nation except the United States . . . our gigantic physical power in natural resources, credit, machine technology, transport and communication facilities . . . the historic resourcefulness and high level of intelligence among our people . . . the deep-running sense of the American Way of enlightened self-interest and sincere humanitarianism . . . the unique "classlessness" of our history . . . the current awakening of the American public mind to the fact that nationalism, imperialism, and isolationism, must be done away with if humanity is to be able to live in an abundant society . . . in short, the widening vista of the good life which could be lived now around the earth. All these factors, taken together, say to me that Now is the Moment and America is the fulcrum around which we shall move the social world.

There are moments in history
    when Today is merely Today . . .
    inert, unchanging . . .
When no mustering of energies
Can prod man out of his inertia.

Then comes the moment
    when Tomorrow is Today,
When the flux is at free flow.
Then Man is Captain of his Soul
And the principle of the effective human act
    Works in a world at social crisis.

GENTLEMEN, THIS IS OUR MOMENT—IF!

Eight

THE BATTLE FOR CONSENT:

My Dear Colleagues in Education:

The time has come for some plain talk about ourselves, for our special technology lies at the nub of the present crisis. Education is so indispensable to the carrying on of a democratic society that if our fathers could have truly educated our generation, in addition to making us literate, we could probably have prevented this major social upheaval. We should have foreseen and warded off the dangers before they bowled us over. To say this does not minimize our elders' achievement in building the legal and physical structure of the world's first system of universal education. A good job it was—achieved in two generations and at the very moment when they were also clearing a virgin continent and setting up the first potentially efficient production system in man's history. Little wonder that they could not both found the new culture and critically appraise it as they built it. Even our great creatives—Veblen, Peirce, Sullivan—after having actually had concrete experience of the new culture, encountered almost insurmountable difficulties in laying bare its conceptual roots.

Nevertheless it is a fact that this generation has inherited baffling problems of social reconstruction in which we in professional education must play a leading role. That has been increasingly evident for some years and I have long considered making some simple and direct proposals to you about it. To save space and your time and to rivet our total attention I have decided to write "open letters" to a few (specially chosen ones) among us who are now in focal positions to act quickly and with nation-wide influence.

First, in this letter to all in education, I wish to lay a foundation for the specifics of the other ones. For economy, I shall have to assume in writing these letters that my readers have read the preceding pages of this book.

✦ ✦ ✦

When the armistices in Today's War Abroad occur, two great battles will be taken up in Tomorrow's War At Home—the Battle for Distribution and the Battle for Consent. The two are really one, for in a democracy social changes can be brought about under the leadership of government only when government "derives its just powers from the consent of the governed." Here I shall say little more about the Battle for Distribution, relying on my earlier documentation from the nationally consti-tuted key group at our capital.

Winning the Battle for Consent is primarily our func-tion, for consent is given only when the governed *under-stand* their deep-lying conditions and issues. It is true of course, that consent also requires that the rights of the people shall be guaranteed in written charters of liberty . . . that these shall be implemented by adequate eco-nomic conditions . . . and that the machinery of the popular suffrage shall not only be provided but shall ac-tually be operated to permit all of the adult population to vote—no hampering "poll taxes," no color line, no property line, no party line to interfere. But the real nub of consent is that the people shall understand and that understanding can be developed in our complicated society only through education—education conceived in the very broadest and deepest sense.

If we need support from our social-engineering statesmen, we have it in their warning that one of the two foci of the Battle for Distribution is psychological and hence educational. They insist that in order to make over our social-economic system in ways now required of us to keep it running, our people have first to make up their minds. Recall Alvin Hansen's dictum: "We have to make up our minds as a nation that we will not permit a postwar depression to overwhelm us." It is said by many people in Washington who are in a position to know, that the two great steps of (1) leading in world reconstruction and (2) running the economic system at full employment in peace time will not be taken unless at least a large vocal minority of the people tell the Congress and the Executive in unmistakable tones and words that they want it so. The chief problem before us therefore is the building of a vast public support for the plans in progress to which I referred in Chapter VI.

The solemn fact is that, although a few of our most discerning statesmen and a tiny spearhead of alert citizens and students see and are stating clearly the grave task before the nation, there is no large vocal minority telling the Congress that they want something done about it. How can there be when most of the people lack the facts with which to make up their minds? How can there be unless we, who are responsible for assembling the facts and for organizing study and discussion machinery, get the facts before them? That the people are now getting a censored, distorted report and a biased interpretation of events, trends, and issues from the press, radio, and newsreel is generally agreed upon by students of public opinion. As a single example of withholding the facts, witness the failure of 99 per cent of the mass-circulation newspapers either to print or to comment sincerely and objectively upon the Vice-President's "Price of a Free World Victory" speech. It is true that one New York newspaper, *PM*, printed it twice and commented on it frequently but even the *New York Times*, famous for its printing of the full texts of distinguished documents and addresses, ignored it. Meanwhile the McCormick-Patterson-Hearst press, reaching not less than 10,000,000 citizens daily, censors and distorts every progressive event in a manner that is downright dangerous to the morale of this nation.

As a consequence it is a conservative estimate to say that far less than one million Americans—I think it is nearer half a million—are today in the process of making up their minds by considering the actual facts of the most crucial issues of modern history. How many should there be? No accurate forecasts can be given, but I should say that a vocal minority of 10,000,000 would coalesce enough others to elect a Congress of intelligent, welfare-minded, and free-world-minded representatives.

With many of you I have worked at these tasks for a full quarter of a century. During the past ten years my mind has not been off this problem of building a clear progressive climate of opinion for a single day. I give it to you as my most considered judgment that if the trunk lines of communication (I name them in the following letters) were made available to us we could build quickly a vocal minority of American citizens—yes, ten million —who would understand the present problems and could make themselves heard. We could get America to speak the message of the Great Tradition . . . to make it clear that the Exploitive Tradition has run its course. In two years time—and few believe that the war will begin to stop before that—we could build intelligent support for efficient post-war leadership.

In the following letters to persons who could lead powerfully in this enterprise I have given a brief of the kind of program that seems to me to be required.

THE HONORABLE FRANKLIN DELANO ROOSEVELT
PRESIDENT OF THE UNITED STATES
WASHINGTON, D. C.

DEAR MR. PRESIDENT:

Because of your magnificent statesmanship in assembling and guiding many of the forces that are now poised for the Battle for Distribution, we in education turn to you for leadership in our battle—the Battle for Consent.

Whatever we are to do to build supporting public opinion for your plans-in-progress for winning the peace must be done quickly. Programs must be designed at once and social machinery set up and pushed into motion. But the leadership lies in the national government—it has the sovereignty, can provide the social machinery, and muster the creative energies so sorely needed at this moment. No private individuals or organizations can do it. The history of the fine attempts of our liberal spearhead groups during the past forty years proves beyond dispute that private efforts to redirect social trend succeed only when given a generation of time for the effects to be felt. But we do not have a generation to bring to the American people the facts that will enable them to make up their minds about world leadership and full employment at home. We do not have even a decade. We have only the next few years while the war against military fascism is on. The mind of the American people must be made up by the time the armistices arrive. So I repeat: whatever is done must be done quickly and whatever is to be done quickly must be done under the leadership of national government. And so—in spite of the staggering burden which you are now carrying—we turn to you.

Perhaps you will say: "I gave John Studebaker that job." You did . . . it's his job, but John can't do it without your aid. The chief reason is the everpresent bottle neck which throttles every progressive move—namely, a chonic inertia and hesitation among our educational administrators to deal with things that really matter. As a profession we have been told by the lay representatives on our "Boards" and by the prestige sectors of the communities that education is to follow, not to lead . . . to inform, not to appraise critically . . . to describe, not to reconstruct . . . to review history and principles but not analyze contemporary conditions and controversial issues.

"How absurd!" you say. It is . . . and many among us have said so for a long, long time . . . without much effect. The inevitable result of the impact of such a climate of opinion of three generations of educational administration is to create a vast timidity and inferiority in our official leadership. The harmful effects of all this did not show up glaringly in placid times. But now that we confront a deep crisis in every phase of our world culture, now that social invention and courageous initiative are positively demanded, our educational leaders are baffled, even frightened. They are so practised in "thinking little" that they are helpless when a New Day with novel and frightening problems bursts upon them requiring them to "think big." Under such conditions they must be bucked up and you are probably the only person who can do it.

Look candidly at the situation. Our President and his innermost Council of Design and Administration are moving swiftly to beat the greatest crisis of modern history by meeting it more than half way. They "think big." They tell the people straight out:

—that we need not have a depression when peace comes,
—that we can run the economic system in peace-time as in war-time on a full-employment-*at-abundance-level* (I insist on the "at-abundance-level" qualifying clause),
—that the present bottle neck in finance-capitalism must be gotten rid of, that credit must flow freely to all worthy producers, little or big,
—that a people can afford whatever it can produce,
—that with our giant resources we need not fear the national debt,
—that if private initiative does not act promptly to maintain full-employment, government must act, even if that means to interject social capital into the system,
—that the only possible way out for us as well as for other peoples is for the Americans to lead and nurse a sick world, running the economic system at full tilt and giving away our products for a considerable time to come.

Now the study and thinking of a fair-sized brigade of educational leaders—superintendents, professors, teachers, text-book writers, curriculum makers—have led them to much the same conclusions and affirmations. More than all else they crave a chance to teach these great ideas to their high school youths and to the prospective teachers in the colleges of education.

But even though you and your key group are beginning to make these heartening pronouncements, few of the people are hearing them. As I have just said in the letter to my colleagues, while we need not less than ten million working at the problem of understanding the key ideas of the New World that will be ushered in when peace comes, the total number who are doing so doesn't exceed a million. With your help we can get the ten million—yes, twenty million—at the job; without it the administrators of education, while they will help vigorously to win the war abroad, are going to do practically nothing about winning the peace at home. Count on it . . . they will wait for a "green light" from persons in high places.

So again I come back to you and to John Studebaker. With your help now John could put on a nation-wide campaign of publications, broadcasts, forums, panels, round tables, and study-discussion clubs that in two years would give the people the facts needed to understand and appraise the great concepts which lie at the nub of our crisis. But without your vigorous collaboration John just isn't going to do it. If you ask "Why?" I must reply that the answer is found largely in the general blockage in Washington against progressive developments in edu-

cation. For years something has been stymying all effort
to rebuild American education to fit the demands of the
new world. Distinguished progressives have tried repeatedly to get national leadership for worthy enterprises
from Washington's high places; almost never have they
been able to get it. Why?

I think part of the fault is yours, Mr. President, for you
have never displayed a vigorous interest in the mature
up-building of education in this country. Consider, for
example, the recent pronouncements in which you seem
to make adult education synonymous with eliminating
adult illiteracy. It is a well-known fact that illiteracy is
still disgracefully large and it must and will be eliminated,
but that constitutes an almost negligible part of the vast
task of adult education. In these four "open letters" I am
trying to indicate succinctly what that task really is and
what an indispensable role you have in it.

To break the Washington bottle neck which has held
back American education, there is one major step that
you and only you can take now, Mr. President, and that
is—to create an "Office of Education for Peace." At
present we have an "Office for Education for War." It
is doing a good job of organizing the nation's teachers
and administrators to help win the war abroad. It is possible that under you it could become a powerful instrument to help win the peace and I strongly urge you to
give John Studebaker a chance to do that. But you should
appraise his results promptly and, if they do not affect
the country quickly, a powerful new Office devoted
solely to winning the peace should be created. But even
that will be of little use unless the Office is given unlim-

ited resources—a budget running into millions to reach ten, twenty, thirty million Americans day after day, week after week, without let-up.

But above all else, Mr. President, you must help put an end to the fear and inertia in our profession—for no one else can do it. Make it absolutely clear to the Commissioner that he has complete autonomy; that he can try anything within reason at least once; that he is really the Chief-of-Staff of the forces that are fighting the War-at-Home over a free, abundant, and creative world; that conventional routine ways of doing things are not wanted; that he is expected to create, to assemble the inventive "educational" brains of the entire country— wherever they are found, in the Center-to-Left as in the Center-to-Right; that he has to "think big" for the New Day is big—too big for the old little ways; that no issue —if it is a real issue before our people—is too controversial, no idea is too "dangerous," to be brought out into the open and discussed. Whoever guides the Peace Offensive must believe in his bones that America can lead in building a world of economic and spiritual abundance, and morning, noon, and night must act to convince ten, twenty, thirty million Americans of it.

Let Washington make it clear that there shall be no more appeasing in education!

I may seem to be too vigorous. Well, the times demand vigor. They demand strong clear words and you and your associates can give them and you can put spirit into our profession so we can give them. I can assure you that without your governmental guarantees few educators in America are going to incur the displeasure of the Center-to-Right that exerts a dominating influence over our schools. However, you, through John Studebaker, can give them government's guarantee of security. I repeat emphatically: government must speak to every sector of the American people—and that includes the educators—in no uncertain tones and words, guaranteeing them security if they will work for the new world of abundance. In the same way that it guarantees worthy investors, guarantees worthy job seekers, guarantees worthy home makers, so it must guarantee security to every worthy student, administrator, teacher, writer who in the American democratic spirit goes out to teach the ideas of an abundant America, fully-employed at a high standard of living, and leading a free world.

THE HONORABLE JOHN STUDEBAKER
U. S. COMMISSIONER OF EDUCATION
WASHINGTON, D. C.

DEAR JOHN:

You have been on my mind a lot this summer, especially now that I have come to the conclusion of my book for that brings me to your leadership in our Battle for Consent. I trust deeply that the President will take on the task—in addition to the dreadful burden he is carrying—of helping you to build a great offensive to win the peace. You are already doing the prior job of harnessing up the country's educational team to help win the war abroad. That was the thing to do first and we know that the members of our profession will acquit themselves splendidly as hard-working, sacrificing patriots. But fine and necessary as that is, it still isn't enough, for we fight two wars. As I have said earlier:

To speak of the peace now is to win the war—
the two wars . . .
Tomorrow's war at home
as well as Today's war abroad

You are leading the teachers in fighting Today's-War-Abroad. You must also lead them in fighting Tomorrow's-War-at-Home which will start up again full force when the armistices come.

We are fighting the Common Man's Battle for Consent and you are elected "General" to lead it. And remember . . . it's now or never, so far as this century of the common man is concerned . . . Now is the moment.

This Battle for Consent must be fought exactly as the President and his lieutenants are fighting Hitler—by an all-out total war. But our war . . . to win the Peace . . . is not against guns and bodies; it is against moods, minds, wills. It is against ignorance, indifference, vacillation . . . against prejudice and selfish intrenched interests. It is against willingness to appease, against willingness to accept half a loaf or even a crust instead of the whole loaf which our resources guarantee. And it is a war against a bigotry and race hatred—a war to get the people to implement that word "all" in the Declaration's line—"all men are created equal."

Being a war against minds it can be won only by minds —the best minds you can discover by combing the entire country. By "best" I mean creative, ingenious, flexible . . . and I mean broadly and deeply informed, rigorously trained and practiced in the art of organization . . . and I mean minds buttressed by brave moods for the tasks ahead will require courage as well as brains. In education we need minds that can "think big" to match the "think big" men in the politico-economic branches of the key group that is assembling in Washington.

Your task is nothing less than that of assembling a national council on adult education such as we have never known before. Not only must the members be prepared to think new and think big to meet the novel and gigantic problems that confront us; the personnel must also be diverse enough in social philosophy and in experience and knowledge to organize an offensive of tremendous scope and diversity. Every national channel of communication must be employed to speak to our people—the press in all its ramifications . . . the radio and its round tables and forums . . . the movies and newsreel services . . . the schools and colleges . . . the churches . . . the public lay rostrum . . . the social organizations . . . the art museums, schools, and institutes . . . the existing planning agencies . . . and a whole array of new ones to be invented. Experts familiar with the special techniques and potentialities of each of these must be brought into our army corps—even drafted into it if necessary to get the nation's best.

I am convinced that we can do this educational job of winning the peace if you are given a real war budget and the President will make clear to you that you have a green light to go the limit in your campaign. But to do it means not only having a galaxy of stars to create the designs, but also being able to launch an all-out campaign over every trunk line of communication in this country. It means a nation-wide barrage of ideas and attitudes that will reach every city, town, and hamlet—a barrage day after day, month after month, not letting up for years to come. It means that government must get us access to those national radio and movie newsreel chains . . . access to the movie houses . . . access to syndicated space in newspapers . . . access to two hundred thousand secondary and college teachers and their class rooms and their curricula. It means that government must be ready to print and sell at a nickel or a dime hundreds of pamphlets and bulletins in ten million lots.

This job is right up your alley, John. You can create for the nation—multiplied a thousand fold—what you, as Superintendent did for Des Moines. I shall never forget or cease to give thanks for your program in adult education—the very kind of thing we have just been discussing —community-wide forums, study and discussion groups. You got the whole place excited about finding the real roots of the social-economic impasse. They certainly were not afraid of controversial issues in Des Moines in the early 1930s—had them right out in the open where they should be with the lime-light of public scrutiny and study playing full on them. It was a grand job, and when you went to Washington in 1933 as "Commissioner of Education" for the American People we threw our hats in the air and said "Now something really important will happen!"

Well, John, we waited . . . and waited . . . but mighty little happened. It seemed to your liberal friends across the country that something in Washington got you slowed down. The conventional Office of Education routine was continued . . . some minor novelties were launched—all good enough in their way but not the things needed by a bewildered and baffled people caught in the world's worst depression. To this day I haven't been able to make out what held you back. Other administrators have gone to work under the aegis of the key group in Washington and come out of it upstanding fighters for an abundant world. Why not the American Commissioner of Education and his associates? Why not? The question is important and some time, for the sake of the record, should be answered by those who know.

But for the moment it's not important. Let's put all we've got on this task of doing for America what you did for Des Moines. Get a picture of what it would look like:

—A million study-discussion clubs—yes, a million . . . one in every one of the neighborhoods of America . . . organized around alert citizens, including teachers, as leaders.

—Ten thousand weekly forums . . . panels . . . round tables in the school houses and theatres and municipal auditoriums of the nation . . . Center-to-Right and Center-to-Left on the same platform—just as you did at Des Moines, John.

—National radio hook-ups of similar "Town Meetings," panels, round tables, luncheon and dinner meetings, listened to and discussed by a million study clubs.

—Four Minute or Ten Minute men and news reel shorts in the movie houses of the nation every week in the year.

—The curricula of a hundred thousand senior high school and college classes made over to incorporate this same study of winning the peace.

And . . . as for materials! This campaign requires a pamphlet—bulletin-article-book-writing program that would dwarf anything that has ever been dreamed of in this or any other country. The nation's finest novelists, poets, essayists, columnists, and other publicists, drafted to write. Drafted, I say. The nation's scholars in the social sciences—economics, politics, government, history, sociology, social psychology, and public opinion—drafted to organize topics, to outline material, to collaborate with the professional writers in preparing books, pamphlets, bulletins, articles printed by government printing presses and syndicated at cost throughout the country.

We have merely lifted the curtain a bit, John, on the kind of scene that you could stage in our educational drama in the next few years. This really is our moment to make dreams come true. Long have we looked toward a millennial day when the American citizenry would become intelligent and alert, when understanding and tolerance would be abroad in the land. The dawn of that New Day is now on the horizon and it seems possible for us to usher it in to throw fuller light on our problems.

To The American Superintendents of Schools; Especially to such Community Leaders as:

C. B. GLENN	JOHN A. SEXTON
HEROLD C. HUNT	ALEXANDER J. STODDARD
ARTHUR K. LOOMIS	WILLIS A. SUTTON
WORTH MCCLURE	A. L. THRELKELD
W. H. PILLSBURY	JULIUS E. WARREN

CARLETON WASHBURNE

My dear Friends:

I come now to your leadership in the Battle for Consent. In a very real sense you are the Major Generals on John Studebaker's staff—the key men in the building of understanding in the communities of America. To the extent that you move out in advance . . . or drift . . .

or stand aloof . . . so will most of the teachers and children and many of the parents. If America's federal and regional Councils of Design and Reconstruction are to be based on a virile local leadership it will be because you more than any other persons will have created it. Moreover your influence extends far beyond the borders of your own local communities; what you preach and practice is broadcast over the entire country.

I am keenly aware that you administrators will fight the coming Battle for Consent under grave difficulties. Your offices will necessarily be in the very center of social conflict, a barrage of persuasion and coercion playing around you most of the time. The Center-to-Left, although without much political power, will urge you to lead vigorously in reconstructing the schools to fit a new world—even to use the schools to "rebuild the social order." The dominant groups within the Center-to-Right will not only hold you back but will try to use you and the schools to turn the social order back to the "normalcy" of an out-moded day. The racketeering fringe of the Far-Right, consisting of false patriots and reactionary "little economic royalists" will deliberately try to build up fear and social hysteria in your communities and even to destroy the democratic process itself. As I write (autumn 1942) there is a superficial lull in the domestic battle. But it is only an apparent armistice; witness the unceasing venom of the McCormick-Patterson-Hearst press, the die-hards of Congress, the subterranean activities of the Father Coughlin fascist type of activity and the current bulletins of Merwin K. Hart's personal organization—The New York State Economic Council —all of which continues the ten-year attack on the federal program at Washington and on everything progressive in the schools.

Democratic educational leaders find themselves in a bad situation on such a confused battle front. And when the armistices come in the war abroad it is going to be worse—unless we take effective measures now toward dissipating it. The incipient fascism that is latent in most of our communities today could quickly and virulently infect the social blood stream of our country; it could utterly strangle our treasured democratic process and turn your teachers and youth into fearsome parrots of an authoritarian regime. All that is possible unless the devoted defenders of American democracy quickly inject into the social blood stream a powerful anti-toxin.

Only the brilliant light of thorough study and discussion—the giant program of adult education which I sketched in my letter to John Studebaker—promises to be strong enough to kill the fascist microbes in their incipient stages. In that process you, my friends, are literally the keys to the doors of understanding to the American people. Around you as Directors can be created Community Councils of Design and Reconstruction and a two-fold mechanism of Forums and Study-Discussion Clubs. I have no doubt that in some of your communities the present Board of Education could serve as an effective nucleus of the central council. But in most cases its personnel will need to be greatly expanded on the side of talented youth and of imaginative and forceful leaders of labor, of Negro, and other minority groups, if the Council is to be a real cross section of the creative ability of the community. Moreover, the Center-to-Left, generally missing or occupying a subordinate role, will have to be given a place coördinate with the Center-to-Right. If this is not done the whole enterprise will be abortive and our Battle for Consent will be lost.

Now your position in the nation-wide program of study is not a casual or minor one. It is focal. Indeed it would be difficult to build a truly effective national program of adult education without your local direction in 20,000 communities. John Studebaker can assign it, finance it, set up all the central activities of broadcasts, movies, lectures, Town Meetings, Panels, Round Tables, what not, but it will fall absolutely flat unless you in your respective communities get the ten million, yes twenty million citizens to listen, study, think, and discuss.

If understanding and tolerance are to be abroad in our beloved land millions of our citizens must come to grips with the key ideas that underlie the two major problems discussed in this book: the problem of leading in world rehabilitation and the problem of full-employment-at-abundance-level. It will help little for our people merely to chant new slogans in place of old ones; a nebulous palaver about a new world of full employment and abundance will fall far short of building understanding and tolerance. But ten thousand forums and a million study groups working at those two problems systematically with clear documented materials can do it. And you personally are the Key Men to create these forums and groups. You can build understanding in ten million minds by giving the facts that clarify the ideas and document the problems. And this means bringing controversial issues before the American people.

Moreover, most of the ideas and issues at stake in the Battle for Consent are fairly simple. I cite ten that, if grasped by the Ten Million, would win the peace:

—The idea that every nation on earth must be disarmed . . . that all armaments be pooled and administered by a central world "police force."
—The idea that in worth and dignity, in sovereignty of personality all individuals and peoples of the earth are equal and there shall be no more imperial exploitation of the weak by the strong.
—The idea of the fragile interdependence of our people with the other industrialized peoples of the earth . . . so that most of the human race now stand or fall together.
—The idea that we have now on this continent the makings of a great civilization—the abundant life . . . that things are plentiful, not scarce, as our fathers said.
—The idea that a people as rich as ours, need not fear a debt, even as large and growing as is ours.
—The idea that the farms and factories can safely be run at full employment in peace-time as well as in war.
—The idea that the government can take vigorous steps to prevent a depression at the close of Today's War Abroad.
—The idea that a people can afford whatever it can produce.

In all this dramatic study no task is more important than that of developing the conviction that the Americans in company with other modern peoples are now rethinking and redefining their primary concepts to fit the new world that is being ushered in.

I recognize that I am repeating what I said in the earlier parts of this book but I am doing it only to make sure that I am clear. This time we must not fail to win the peace, otherwise all this dreadful blood letting will have been in vain. The only way to make doubly sure is to see that our giant program of adult education is concentrated directly on the heart of our crisis; it must not dodge a single necessary condition or factor, or ignore a single controversial issue. It must bring to the people the facts necessary to enable them to make up their minds that . . .

> Tomorrow is Today . . . that
> The mammoth glacier of social trend
>   taking movement down the Valley of History
>   can be diverted by man
> Into pathways toward Tomorrow.

APPENDIX

major sources for supplementary reading for Chapters III and IV: W. T. Stace: *The Destiny of Western Man* (Reynal and Hitchcock, 1942), James Feibleman: *Positive Democracy* (University of North Carolina Press, 1940), Pitirim Sorokin, head of the Sociology Department at Harvard University: *The Crisis of Our Age* (1941) and *Man and Society in Calamity* (1942, both Dutton) based on his four research volumes, *Social and Cultural Dynamics* (American Book Company, 1937-41), and Waldo Frank: *Chart for Rough Water* (Doubleday, 1941).

The "new historians" on both sides of the Atlantic are building a great library of original interpretations of our society. The contribution of the British School is well typified by R. H. Tawney's *Religion and the Rise of Capitalism* (Harcourt Brace, 1926), J. A. Hobson: *Evolution of Modern Capitalism* (London, 1926) and—particularly for the interpretation of the deep-running trends—Arnold J. Toynbee's six-volume *Study of History* (Oxford). Also see the publications of such other professors of the London School of Economics and Political Science as Harold Laski: *The Rise of Liberalism* (Harper, 1936) and G. D. H. Cole's thirty-odd volumes, the most recent being *Europe, Russia, and the Future* (Macmillan, 1942). The American school of new historians was really launched by Thorstein Veblen through his *Theory of the Leisure Class* (1899), *The Instinct of Workmanship* (1914), *The Engineers and the Price System* (1919), etc. For his contemporaries and immediate successors, see especially F. J. Turner: *The Frontier in American History* (Holt, 1920); James Harvey Robinson: *The Mind in the Making* (Harper, 1921) and *The Human Comedy* (Harper, 1937); Charles and Mary Beard's four-volume *Rise of American Civilization*, viz: I. *The Agricultural Era, The Industrial Era, America in Mid-Passage,* and *The American Spirit;* Harry Elmer Barnes: *An Intellectual and Cultural History of the Western World* (Cordon, 1937), *Economic History of the Western World* (Harcourt, Brace, 1937), and such other studies as those of William I. Thomas and George H. Mead.

CHAPTERS V AND VI

1. PROPOSED ALTERNATIVE FORMS OF
WORLD ORGANIZATION

The abundance of material devoted to the topic of world political organization is best analyzed in terms of the scope of territory or political unit dealt with. The proposals range from the completely "Isolationist-America-First" view and the "Continental America" position to a variety of regional and "World Federation" plans. I list them succinctly indicating the sources of publication in which plans and principles can be found:

I. *No Plan at All*—Extreme Isolation . . . "America First" . . . Thinking and action based on no change in theory since George Washington's "no entangling alliances." Represented by the speeches of Hamilton Fish, Clare Hoffman, Howard K. Smith, Martin Dies, John Rankin, Stephen Day, Eugene Cox, Leland Ford, Dewey Short, Joseph Starnes, J. P. Thomas, C. W. Brooks, W. Lee O'Daniel. See *Congressional Record* for almost any day in past year.

II. *The Continental America "Plan."* Best represented and defended perhaps in the decade of writing by one of America's most devoted and loyal citizens and one of the most liberal and profound students of modern cultures—Charles A. Beard. Perhaps the fullest presentation of the point of view is to be found in his *Open Door at Home* (Macmillan, 1934).

III. *The Western Hemisphere Plan.* See George Jaffin: *New World Constitutional Harmony: A Pan-Americanadian Panorama* (Columbia Law Review, 1942) for a discussion of Hemispheric Union based on ideological commonality.

IV. *Anglo-Saxon Leadership (Britain and America).*

a. Center-to-Left: Clarence Streit: *Union Now* (1940) and *Union Now with Britain* (Harper, 1941) proposes a union of English-speaking democracies, with a constitution modeled on the American system of federal union.

b. Center-to-Right: *Fortune* Editors: *The United States*

in a New World—I. *Relations with Britain* (May 1942)
. . . II. *Pacific Relations* (August 1942) provides an economic structure for policing, protection, and development of the world. This appears to be perilously close to Anglo-Saxon imperialism, with national "normalcy," *laissez faire*-private-enterprise as the economic framework.

V. *Regional Plans*. Step-by-step graduated federalism of the world on the order of TVA regionalism in the United States, such as outlined by George Soule and *The New Republic* Editors in "The Lessons of Last Time," (*The New Republic*, February 2, 1942).

VI. *Various So-Called "Good Neighbor" Plans*, depending heavily on the "Good Neighbor" policy of the United States and Latin America, sometimes called the Good Will plans in which the victor is willing to make economic sacrifices in order to construct a durable peace. See Lionel Curtis: *World Order* . . . Glenn Clark: *Two or Three Gathered Together* . . . Roswell Barnes: *A Christian Imperative, Our Contribution to World Order* . . . Louis Adamic: *Two-Way Passage* (Harper, 1941) . . . Hoover and Gibson: *Problems of Lasting Peace* (Doubleday, 1942).

VII. *The United Nations Approach*. See the World Citizens Association reports:
The United Nations, What They Are, What They May Become and *The United Nations on the Way* in which Henri Bonnet discusses the organization of a United Nations Political Council.

VIII. *World Federation Plans,* including Regional Federations.

a. Economic plans: Hans Heymann: *Plans for Permanent Peace* (1941) and *Justice for All* (1943; both Harper), a proposal for a Bank of Nations and Otto Tod Mallery: *Economic Order and Durable Peace* (Harper, 1943); abstract in *International Conciliation* (November 1942).

b. Complete World Federation structure . . . guaranteeing disarmament, providing for economic structures and operation: Ely Culbertson: *The World Federation Plan* (obtainable from World Federation, Inc., 16A East 62nd Street, New York City).

IX. *"League of Nations" Plans*. Based on The League of Nations; proposals for modifications in the light of its history with two groups working independently, each composed of persons active in its constitution and operation.

a. Commission for the Study of Organization of Peace: Led by Messrs. J. T. Shotwell and Charles Eichelberger . . . two preliminary reports in *International Conciliation* (April 1941 and April 1942) . . . tentative blueprints in preparation, ready Spring or Summer, 1943.

b. Institute on World Organization, Washington, D. C. This group is largely composed of members of the former Secretariat of the League of Nations. See their Symposium on *World Organization*, (published under the auspices of the American Council on Public Affairs) and C. J. Hambro: *How to Win the Peace* (Lippincott, 1942).

OPPOSED TO THE FOREGOING—

X. *Geopolitics*. Rule by the victors . . . in the case of the United Nations this is supposed to mean a "democratic" kind of nationalism and "benevolent imperialism." In the case of the Fascist-Dictatorship nations it means ruthless "Geopolitics"—domination of the earth by the Master Race, governed by the Master Class. For the Germanic brand see Karl Haushofer: *Power and Earth* . . . for the Anglo-Saxon, Nicholas Spykman: *America's Strategy in World Politics* (Harcourt, Brace, 1942). See Hans W. Weigert: *Generals and Geographers* (Oxford, 1942) or Robert Strausz-Hupé: *Geopolitics* (Putnam, 1942) for clear and incisive interpretations of the whole problem and trend.[1]

[1] Sources for additional study of the problem:
Foreign Policy Reports: "What Americans Think about Post-War Reconstruction" (October 1, 1942) and "As Britain Sees the Post-War World" (October 15, 1942)
G. D. H. Cole: *Europe, Russia and the Future* (Macmillan, 1942)
Edward Carr: *Conditions of Peace* (Macmillan, 1942)

2. DOMESTIC ECONOMIC RECONSTRUCTION

The research on the problem of how to run the economic system at a full-employment, abundance level, first motivated by the Brookings Institution (Moulton, *et al.*) and the National Survey Engineers (Loeb, *et al.*), has now reached broad proportions. We can be certain that in the years immediately ahead, both the grown up and youth population of our country will have sufficient data with which to make up their minds that we can now provide every human being in America with a high level national minimum.

In the following list I have classified some of the more important analyses according to the aspect of the problem studied:

Full Employment at
Abundance Level

William H. Stead: *Democracy against Unemployment* (Harper, 1942)

National Resources Planning Board: *After Defense—What* (1941) . . . *After the War—Full Employment* (1942) . . . *Post-War Planning* (1942)

Office of War Information: *Toward New Horizons* (speeches by Wallace, Welles, Winant, and Perkins)

Alvin Hansen and Guy Greer: "Toward Full Use of Our Resources" (*Fortune*, November 1942)

The American Way is
a "Mixed Economy"

Lewis Corey: *The Unfinished Task* (Viking, 1942)

Lewis Lorwin: *Economic Consequences of the Second World War* (Random House, 1941)

P. E. Corbett: *Post-War Worlds* (Farrar, 1942)

R. N. Coudenhove-Kalergi: *Pan Europe* (1926—later adapted to a United Nations victory.)

J. B. Condliffe: *Agenda for a Post-War World* (Norton, 1942)

George Galloway: *Planning for America* (Holt, 1941).
An indispensable source book is Galloway's *Post-War
Planning in the United States* (Twentieth Century
Fund, 1942).

Edwin G. Nourse: *Price-Making in a Democracy* (Brookings Institution, 1942-43). Writing in the background
of the social engineers, Nourse defines the role of a
modified "free enterprise" after the war.

Alfred Bingham: *The Techniques of Democracy* (Duell,
Sloan and Pearce, 1942). On the role of government.

James Burnham: *The Managerial Revolution* (John Day,
1941). On the role of management.

*A National Minimum: The
Budget of Our Needs and Resources*

Chase: *Goals for America*

William Beveridge: *Social Insurance and Allied Services*
(Macmillan, 1942)

National Resources Planning Board: See forthcoming report, 1943

Fortune Magazine, Supplement to December, 1942: "The
Domestic Economy"

The National Resources Planning Board has been making
and publishing positive studies of the use and control of our
resources for eight years. Among them the major reports
are: *Technological Trends and National Planning, Consumer Incomes in the United States, Problems of a Changing
Population, Economic Effects of the Federal Public Works
Expenditures, Development of Resources and Stabilization
of Employment in the United States, Our Cities—Their
Role in the National Economy, Housing: the Continuing
Problem.* (Pamphlets summarizing these reports can be secured from the Superintendent of Public Documents at ten
cents each.) The Board now fills the important function of
serving as clearing house for all available significant plans
and programs for post-war reconstruction, and its current
reports are of utmost importance.

In studying domestic post-war reconstruction discussion groups must not miss the book-length interpretations that have been coming for several years from the pens of Washington publicists. From the Center-to-Right comes the valuable *Washington Is Like That* of W. B. Kiplinger (Harper, 1942), who for many years has distributed especially to business men his weekly commentary on world and domestic problems as focused in Washington. From the position of one who was in the New Deal group from its inception in Governor Roosevelt's New York meetings and had a post in the government for a while come Mr. John Franklin Carter's (Jay Franklin) splendid *1940* and *Remaking America* (Houghton Mifflin, 1942). "Pro" though they are, they constitute today about the best brief publicist statement of the aims, changing personnel, pro and con forces in Washington and a summary "history" of the achievements of the first eight years of New Deal government. The middle-of-the-road view, but written with fine objectivity, is found in the ringing *Boom or Bust* of Blair Moody (Duell, Sloan and Pearce, 1942), Washington journalist and columnist ("The Low Down in Washington") since 1933.

Chapter VII

To understand the course of the Great Tradition throughout the three stages of American statement one would be forced to study the lives and the utterances of the outstanding Americans who for a century have been producing it, but an introductory outline to guide that study is at hand in the writings of several American students. Ralph Henry Gabriel's *The Course of American Democratic Thought* (Ronald Press, 1940) is an excellent outline guide to the study of the economic, political, and moral-ethical aspects of the problem. The development of the literary mind is sketched in Vernon Parrington's three-volume *Main Currents in American Thought* (Harcourt, 1927-30) (see especially Vols. II and III for the nineteenth century). The era of rebellion and improvisation which followed the death of

Whitman is powerfully expressed through Van Wyck Brooks' early *America's Coming of Age* (1915, reprinted in *Three Essays on America*, Dutton, 1940) and the first two volumes of his historical study of American literature—*The Flowering of New England* (1936) and *New England: Indian Summer* (1940; both Dutton) . . . and in such selected essays as "The Twilight of Idols" in Randolph Bourne's *Untimely Papers* (1919) and *The History of a Literary Radical* (1920). Perhaps the best statement of the Great Tradition in American writing is that of Waldo Frank as presented in his *Our America* (1919), *Salvos* (1924), *Rediscovery of America* (1929), *In the American Jungle* (1937). That the newest and youngest critic of the American literary mind, Albert Kazin, may prove to be the most astute one is suggested by his current *On Native Grounds* (Reynal and Hitchcock, 1942). For the best critical review of the work of the Symbolists see Edmund Wilson's *Axel's Castle* (Scribner, 1941). One of the most profound analyses and clearest expressions of the long-time view of the development of the creative process in our western civilization is Horace Kallen's two-volume *Art and Freedom* (Duell, Sloan and Pearce, 1942).

The educational strand of American expressive development has been studied by Merle Curti: *The Social Ideas of American Educators* (Scribner, 1935) . . . George Counts: *The American Road to Culture* (John Day, 1930) . . . Counts and others: *Social Foundations of Education* (Scribner, 1934) . . . Harold Rugg: *American Life and the School Curriculum* (Ginn, 1936), and chapters from his *That Men May Understand* (Doubleday, 1941), and from the Third Yearbook of the John Dewey Society: *Democracy and the Curriculum* (Appleton-Century, 1939).

For the creative analysis of the social frontier, especially on the economic-political side, see Joseph Dorfman: *Thorstein Veblen and His America* (Viking, 1934) . . . Harry Elmer Barnes: *The History and the Prospects of the Social Sciences* (Knopf, 1925) . . . Charles Beard: *A Charter for the Social Sciences* (Scribner, 1932) . . . James Harvey Robinson: *The New History* (Macmillan, 1918).

The most incisive exposition of the expressive movement in the graphic and plastic arts has been made by Sheldon Cheney: *Expressionism in Art* (Liveright, 1934); in the modern dance by John Martin: *America Dancing* (Dodge, 1936) and *Introduction to the Dance* (Norton, 1939) . . . Barbara Morgan's "bridge of translation" between plastic dance and graphic photographs: *Martha Graham* (Duell, Sloan and Pearce, 1941) . . . Virginia Stewart, editor: *Modern Dance* (Weyhe, 1935).

On the rise of the new theatre see especially Gordon Craig: *On the Art of the Theatre* (Small, Meynard, 1911) . . . Joseph Wood Krutch: *American Drama since 1918* (Random House, 1939) . . . For the trend toward a national theatre see Norris Houghton: *Advance from Broadway* (Harcourt, 1941) . . . and Hallie Flanagan: *Arena* (Duell, Sloan and Pearce, 1940) for the complex and dramatic story of the attempt to build a federal theatre. Also, don't miss Mordecai Gorelik: *New Theatres for Old* (French, 1941) . . . Roy Mitchell: *Creative Theatre* (Day, 1929) . . . and one of George Jean Nathan's critical books, perhaps the 1942 one: *The Entertainment of a Nation.* (Knopf).

On photography in American life, see Frank, Mumford, and others: *America and Alfred Stieglitz* (Doubleday, 1934) and Beaumont Newhall: *Photography A Short Critical History* (Museum of Modern Art, 1937) for introductory guides; also the entire file of *Camera Work* (1902-1917) for the most profound revelation of creative leadership in the graphic and plastic arts in the period of revolt and improvisation.

The clearest short portrait of developing American culture as expressed through the House of the American is found in Lewis Mumford: *Sticks and Stones* (Liveright, 1924). The readings suggested to accompany Chapter II should also be used in this connection.

On the social gospel movement perhaps the best single analysis is F. Ernest Johnson's *The Social Gospel Reëxamined* (Harper, 1940). On the "neo-orthodoxy" see especially Reinhold Niebuhr: *An Interpretation of Christian Ethics* (Harper, 1937).

INDEX

INDEX